D1314412

Immigration to North America

Asylum Seekers

Frank Wright

Asylum Seekers

Central American Immigrants

Chinese Immigrants

Cuban Immigrants

Indian Immigrants

Mexican Immigrants

Middle Eastern Immigrants

Refugees

Rights & Responsibilities of Citizenship

South American Immigrants

Undocumented Immigration and Homeland Security

Immigration to North America

Asylum Seekers

Frank Wright

Senior Consulting Editor Stuart Anderson
former Associate Commissioner for Policy and Planning,
US. Citizenship and Immigration Services

Introduction by Marian L. Smith, Historian,
U.S. Citizenship and Immigration Services

Introduction by Peter A. Hammerschmidt,
former First Secretary, Permanent Mission of Canada to the United Nations

MASON CREST
PHILADELPHIA

Mason Crest
450 Parkway Drive, Suite D
Broomall, PA 19008
www.masoncrest.com

©2017 by Mason Crest, an imprint of National Highlights, Inc.

All rights reserved. No part of this publication may be reproduced or transmitted in any form or by any means, electronic or mechanical, including photocopying, recording, taping, or any information storage and retrieval system, without permission from the publisher.

Printed and bound in the United States of America.

3 1712 01567 5716

CPSIA Compliance Information: Batch #INA2016.
For further information, contact Mason Crest at 1-866-MCP-Book.

First printing
1 3 5 7 9 8 6 4 2

Library of Congress Cataloging-in-Publication Data

on file at the Library of Congress
ISBN: 978-1-4222-3680-2 (hc)
ISBN: 978-1-4222-8097-3 (ebook)

Immigration to North America series ISBN: 978-1-4222-3679-6

Table of Contents

Introduction: The Changing Face of the United States   6
> by Marian L. Smith

Introduction: The Changing Face of Canada   10
> by Peter A. Hammerschmidt

1. What Is an Asylee   15
2. Immigration and Asylum Policy   29
3. Boatlifts from the Caribbean   43
4. Central America   59
5. The Asylum Law Changes of 1996   69
6. The Asylum Process, Step by Step   79
7. Life in the New World   89
8. Asylum in the Spotlight   93

Series Glossary of Key Terms   102
Further Reading   103
Internet Resources   105
Index   107
Contributors   111

KEY ICONS TO LOOK FOR:

 Words to Understand: These words with their easy-to-understand definitions will increase the reader's understanding of the text, while building vocabulary skills.

 Sidebars: This boxed material within the main text allows readers to build knowledge, gain insights, explore possibilities, and broaden their perspectives by weaving together additional information to provide realistic and holistic perspectives.

 Research Projects: Readers are pointed toward areas of further inquiry connected to each chapter. Suggestions are provided for projects that encourage deeper research and analysis.

 Text-Dependent Questions: These questions send the reader back to the text for more careful attention to the evidence presented there.

 Series Glossary of Key Terms: This back-of-the book glossary contains terminology used throughout this series. Words found here increase the reader's ability to read and comprehend higher-level books and articles in this field.

The Changing Face of the United States

Marian L. Smith, Historian
U.S. Citizenship and Immigration Services

Americans commonly assume that immigration today is very different than immigration of the past. The immigrants themselves appear to be unlike immigrants of earlier eras. Their language, their dress, their food, and their ways seem strange. At times people fear too many of these new immigrants will destroy the America they know. But has anything really changed? Do new immigrants have any different effect on America than old immigrants a century ago? Is the American fear of too much immigration a new development? Do immigrants really change America more than America changes the immigrants? The very subject of immigration raises many questions.

In the United States, immigration is more than a chapter in a history book. It is a continuous thread that links the present moment to the first settlers on North American shores. From the first colonists' arrival until today, immigrants have been met by Americans who both welcomed and feared them. Immigrant contributions were always welcome—on the farm, in the fields, and in the factories. Welcoming the poor, the persecuted, and the "huddled masses" became an American principle. Beginning with the original Pilgrims' flight from religious persecution in the 1600s, through the Irish migration to escape starvation in the 1800s, to the relocation of Central Americans seeking refuge from civil wars in the 1980s and 1990s, the United States has considered itself a haven for the destitute and the oppressed.

But there was also concern that immigrants would not adopt American ways, habits, or language. Too many immigrants might overwhelm America. If so, the dream of the Founding Fathers for United States government and society would be destroyed. For this reason, throughout American history some have argued that limiting or ending immigration is our patriotic duty. Benjamin Franklin feared there were so many German immigrants in Pennsylvania the Colonial Legislature would begin speaking German. "Progressive" leaders of the early 1900s feared that immigrants who could not read and understand the English language were not only exploited by "big business," but also served as the foundation for "machine politics" that undermined the U.S. Constitution. This theme continues today, usually voiced by those who bear no malice toward immigrants but who want to preserve American ideals.

Have immigrants changed? In colonial days, when most colonists were of English descent, they considered Germans, Swiss, and French immigrants as different. They were not "one of us" because they spoke a different language. Generations later, Americans of German or French descent viewed Polish, Italian, and Russian immigrants as strange. They were not "like us" because they had a different religion, or because they did not come from a tradition of constitutional government. Recently, Americans of Polish or Italian descent have seen Nicaraguan, Pakistani, or Vietnamese immigrants as too different to be included. It has long been said of American immigration that the latest ones to arrive usually want to close the door behind them.

It is important to remember that fear of individual immigrant groups seldom lasted, and always lessened. Benjamin Franklin's anxiety over German immigrants disappeared after those immigrants' sons and daughters helped the nation gain independence in the Revolutionary War. The Irish of the mid-1800s were among the most hated immigrants, but today we all wear green on St. Patrick's Day. While a century ago it was feared that Italian and other Catholic immigrants would vote as directed by the Pope, today that controversy is only a vague memory. Unfortunately, some ethnic groups continue their efforts to earn acceptance. The African

Americans' struggle continues, and some Asian Americans, whose families have been in America for generations, are the victims of current anti-immigrant sentiment.

Time changes both immigrants and America. Each wave of new immigrants, with their strange language and habits, eventually grows old and passes away. Their American-born children speak English. The immigrants' grandchildren are completely American. The strange foods of their ancestors—spaghetti, baklava, hummus, or tofu—become common in any American restaurant or grocery store. Much of what the immigrants brought to these shores is lost, principally their language. And what is gained becomes as American as St. Patrick's Day, Hanukkah, or Cinco de Mayo, and we forget that it was once something foreign.

Recent immigrants are all around us. They come from every corner of the earth to join in the American Dream. They will continue to help make the American Dream a reality, just as all the immigrants who came before them have done.

Welcome to the
United States
A Guide for New
Immigrants

UNITED STATES OF AMERICA   Department of Homeland Security

PERMANENT RESIDENT CARD

UNITED STATES OF AMER

We recommend you use this enve
granted your new card.

The Changing Face of Canada

Peter A. Hammerschmidt
former First Secretary, Permanent Mission of Canada to the United Nations

Throughout Canada's history, immigration has shaped and defined the very character of Canadian society. The migration of peoples from every part of the world into Canada has profoundly changed the way we look, speak, eat, and live. Through close and distant relatives who left their lands in search of a better life, all Canadians have links to immigrant pasts. We are a nation built by and of immigrants.

Two parallel forces have shaped the history of Canadian immigration. The enormous diversity of Canada's immigrant population is the most obvious. In the beginning came the enterprising settlers of the "New World," the French and English colonists. Soon after came the Scottish, Irish, and Northern and Central European farmers of the 1700s and 1800s. As the country expanded westward during the mid-1800s, migrant workers began arriving from China, Japan, and other Asian countries. And the turbulent twentieth century brought an even greater variety of immigrants to Canada, from the Caribbean, Africa, India, and Southeast Asia.

So while English- and French-Canadians are the largest ethnic groups in the country today, neither group alone represents a majority of the population. A large and vibrant multicultural mix makes up the rest, particularly in Canada's major cities. Toronto, Vancouver, and Montreal alone are home to people from over 200 ethnic groups!

Less obvious but equally important in the evolution of Canadian immigration has been hope. The promise of a better life lured Europeans and

Americans seeking cheap (sometimes even free) farmland. Thousands of Scots and Irish arrived to escape grinding poverty and starvation. Others came for freedom, to escape religious and political persecution. Canada has long been a haven to the world's dispossessed and disenfranchised—Dutch and German farmers cast out for their religious beliefs, black slaves fleeing the United States, and political refugees of despotic regimes in Europe, Africa, Asia, and South America.

The two forces of diversity and hope, so central to Canada's past, also shaped the modern era of Canadian immigration. Following the Second World War, Canada drew heavily on these influences to forge trailblazing immigration initiatives.

The catalyst for change was the adoption of the Canadian Bill of Rights in 1960. Recognizing its growing diversity and Canadians' changing attitudes towards racism, the government passed a federal statute barring discrimination on the grounds of race, national origin, color, religion, or sex. Effectively rejecting the discriminatory elements in Canadian immigration policy, the Bill of Rights forced the introduction of a new policy in 1962. The focus of immigration abruptly switched from national origin to the individual's potential contribution to Canadian society. The door to Canada was now open to every corner of the world.

Welcoming those seeking new hopes in a new land has also been a feature of Canadian immigration in the modern era. The focus on economic immigration has increased along with Canada's steadily growing economy, but political immigration has also been encouraged. Since 1945, Canada has admitted tens of thousands of displaced persons, including Jewish Holocaust survivors, victims of Soviet crackdowns in Hungary and Czechoslovakia, and refugees from political upheaval in Uganda, Chile, and Vietnam.

Prior to 1978, however, these political refugees were admitted as an exception to normal immigration procedures. That year, Canada revamped its refugee policy with a new Immigration Act that explicitly affirmed Canada's commitment to the resettlement of refugees from oppression. Today, the admission of refugees remains a central part of

Canadian immigration law and regulations.

Amendments to economic and political immigration policy have continued, refining further the bold steps taken during the modern era. Together, these initiatives have turned Canada into one of the world's few truly multicultural states.

Unlike the process of assimilation into a "melting pot" of cultures, immigrants to Canada are more likely to retain their cultural identity, beliefs, and practices. This is the source of some of Canada's greatest strengths as a society. And as a truly multicultural nation, diversity is not seen as a threat to Canadian identity. Quite the contrary—diversity is Canadian identity.

1 WHAT IS AN ASYLEE?

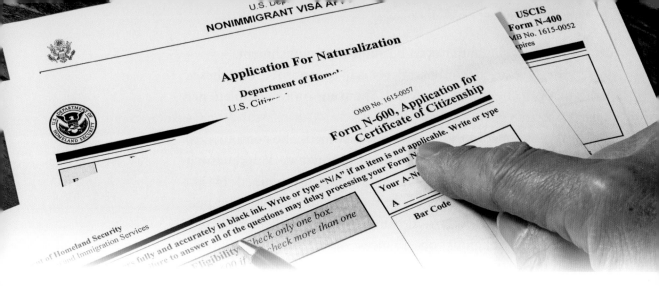

NONIMMIGRANT VISA AP

U.S. Dep

USCIS
Form N-400
MB No. 1615-0052
xpires

Application For Naturalization

Department of Hom

U.S. Citiz

OMB No. 1615-0057

Form N-600, Application for
Certificate of Citizenship

N/A" if an item is not applicable. Write or type

Your A-N

A

Bar Code

fully and accurately in black ink. Write or type
re to answer all of the questions may delay processing your Form N
check only one box.
check more than one
of Homeland Security
and Immigration Services
Eligibility

Like other students pursuing a master's degree, Parvaneh Vahidmanesh had to find a topic for her thesis. Vahidmanesh, who was studying history at Shahid Beheshti University in Tehran, ultimately decided to focus on Iran's Jewish community in the decades after the country's 1979 revolution. That revolution had toppled Iran's monarchy—headed by the shah, or king—and set up a religiously based government, the Islamic Republic of Iran, in its stead. Vahidmanesh wasn't herself Jewish; she followed Islam, the religion of about 99 percent of Iranians. However, she'd been interested in Judaism since age 16, when she found out a family secret: her grandmother had been born Jewish but had been forced, along with all the other Jews in her small town, to convert to Islam.

Parvaneh Vahidmanesh was taken aback by the response to her proposed master's thesis. Most of the history faculty at Shahid Beheshti University vehemently objected to her topic. Eventually, one of Vahidmanesh's professors took her aside and explained why. Iran's Islamic government was extremely sensitive to criticism that it mistreated non-Muslims. To counter such criticism, the government often pointed to what it said was a thriving Iranian Jewish community. If Vahidmanesh's research called the official narrative into question, her thesis would be

◀ A boy rides his bicycle through a bombed-out neighborhood in Homs, Syria, where a devastating civil war has been raging since 2011. The Middle East is one of many turbulent regions around the world that in recent years have produced thousands of victims looking for asylum in the United States or Canada.

censored—and she might even be subject to punishment.

In the face of her advisers' refusal to approve her thesis, Vahidmanesh chose another topic. She went on to complete her master's degree.

But her interest in Iran's Jews never waned. She continued to research the subject. And after she'd graduated, Vahidmanesh teamed with a veteran Iranian photojournalist named Hasan Sarbakhshian to produce a book about Iranian Jews. The pair saw their project as a way to document the daily life, family celebrations, and religious observances of a vanishing culture. Before the creation of the Islamic Republic of Iran in 1979, Iranian Jews numbered perhaps 150,000. Three decades later, according to Iran's government, 25,000 Jews remained in the country. But even that figure, according to independent observers, was wildly inflated: the actual number of Jews living in Iran may have dipped below 10,000.

In early 2008, Vahidmanesh and Sarbakhshian applied to Iran's Ministry of Culture and Islamic Guidance for the neces-

 Words to Understand in This Chapter

asylee—a foreigner who receives asylum in the United States after reaching U.S. soil.

asylum—protection granted by a government to a refugee from another country.

communism—a political and economic system that advocates the elimination of private property, promotes the common ownership of goods, and typically insists that the Communist Party has sole authority to govern.

communist—a follower of communism; relating to or characteristic of communism.

internally displaced—the state of being forced from one's home but still in the country of origin.

lawful permanent resident—a non-citizen legally residing in the United States.

non-refoulement—the principle that a government cannot force people to go back to a country or region where their lives or human rights will be endangered.

refugee—a person outside his or her country of nationality who is unable or unwilling to return because of persecution or a well-founded fear of persecution (and, under U.S. law, who is processed outside the United States for resettlement).

Iranian dissidents protest against the regime in Berlin, 2015. One reason why asylees may not want to return to their home country is that they face the direct threat of violence or war there.

sary permission to publish their book. After a year passed and they'd heard nothing, Sarbakhshian pressed the ministry for a decision. The Iranian government promptly revoked his press credentials and forbade him to work in the country.

Vahidmanesh was called in for questioning by government security officials. They accused her of trying to spread propaganda for Israel and even of spying for that country. They suggested that she'd converted to Judaism. Vahidmanesh was deeply shaken. She knew that a charge of spying could lead to a long prison sentence or possibly to execution. Under Islamic law in Iran, conversion from Islam to another religion was also punishable by death.

Fortunately, in April 2009 Vahidmanesh received an invitation to study at the University of Virginia. She eagerly accepted, coming to the United States on a student visa and hoping her troubles with the Iranian government would blow over.

On June 12, 2009, while Vahidmanesh was in Virginia, Iran held a presidential election. Observers had expected the voting to be close. Yet soon after the polls had closed, Iran's Ministry of the Interior announced a landslide victory for Mahmoud Ahmadinejad, the hard-line incumbent. Ahmadinejad's main challenger, a moderate reformer named Mir Hossein Mousavi, blasted the results as fraudulent. And there were many signs the election had indeed been rigged.

On June 13, hundreds of thousands of Iranians took to the streets of Tehran, Iran's capital city, to protest the elections. Supreme Leader Ayatollah Ali Khamenei—an Islamic cleric and Iran's most powerful official—declared the elections valid. But this did nothing to placate the protestors. Demonstrations quickly spread to other cities, and the crowds grew even larger.

The government tried to suppress the protests with threats and violence. It also tried to minimize the worldwide attention the demonstrations received by prohibiting foreign journalists from leaving their hotels. But cellphone video, recorded and posted online by Iranian protesters, conveyed the magnitude of the unrest. And one video, recorded on June 20, galvanized Iranian opposition to the regime and shocked people across the globe. The video captured the last moments of Neda Agha-Soltan, a 26-year-old philosophy student who'd been walking down a street near a protest in Tehran when she was shot in the chest. Despite the frantic efforts of bystanders who came to her aid, Agha-Soltan bled to death. The killer was apparently a member of the Basij, a militia loyal to Iran's Supreme Leader.

From Virginia, Parvaneh Vahidmanesh was closely following events in her native country. "At that time, I was very emotional," she recalled. "Every day I cried." After she saw the video of Neda Agha-Soltan's death, Vahidmanesh composed a scathing open letter to Supreme Leader Ali Khamenei. On June 29, it was published in the opinion pages of the Wall Street Journal.

In her letter, Vahidmanesh noted that she'd attended elementary school with Khamenei's daughter Boshra. "Neda Soltan, the young innocent girl who was killed on Karegar Avenue, was the same age as me and your daughter," Vahidmanesh wrote.

> She came to the demonstrations with no weapons or knives. All she carried with her was her voice, a voice that cried out in protest against your regime.
>
> Who said the response to such cries is a bullet? You, just like the shah, silence the voices of protestors with gunshots. But don't forget that the shah's harsh methods undid him and caused his regime to fall. Neda has died and her voice will no longer call out to disturb your slumber. But I beg you to consider if [Muhammad, Islam's founding prophet] lived his life the way you have? Islam permits irreligious or secular rulers. It does not permit tyrants. I pity you. All the blood you've spilled has forever stained your 70 years of worship and piety.

After seeing her words in print, Vahidmanesh realized that she wouldn't be able to return to Iran. Her searing attack on the Supreme Leader would almost certainly mark her for retaliation by the government. She applied for asylum in the United States. In September 2009, it was granted.

Asylees and Refugees

The terminology surrounding asylum differs somewhat in the United States and the international community. As used internationally, the term *asylum seeker* denotes a person who claims to be a refugee (defined as someone who has fled his or her country because of a well-founded fear of persecution) but whose claim has yet to be evaluated. An asylum seeker judged to have a valid fear of persecution in his or her home country is a called a refugee.

In the United States, an asylum seeker whose claim is granted is called an asylee. And, under U.S. law, an asylee is distinct from a refugee. The difference involves where the person is processed. A refugee is interviewed outside the United States before being accepted into the country. An asylee must, by definition, already have reached U.S. soil (either legally or without proper documents) before making a request for asylum.

Along with many other countries, the United States has signed the 1967 Protocol Relating to the Status of Refugees, an agreement drawn up by the United Nations that promises rights to refugees. The most important of these rights is called non-refoulement, the assurance that refugees won't be forcibly returned to their countries of origin.

What Is a Refugee?

The 1967 Protocol also establishes detailed criteria for a refugee. According to the document, a refugee is "a person outside of his or her country of nationality who is unable or unwilling to return because of persecution or a well-founded fear of persecution on account of race, religion, nationality, membership in a particular social group, or political opinion."

It's a complex definition, but its specificity is important. The definition sets the standard by which a person is a refugee, and the U.S. government applies this standard to judge asylum cases. To best understand the definition, it helps to examine it step by step.

The first phrase, "outside of his or her country of nationality," simply means someone who has left his or her home country. Those who have left their homes, but not their country, are not refugees; they are called "internally displaced people."

The next phrase presents the condition of the person being "unable or unwilling to return" to the home country. This covers two different situations. In the first, an individual won't return home because he or she fears the government of the home country. Most refugees have this fear. Often, they leave their country because their government is harming them through violence or intimidation.

In the second case, an individual leaves to avoid another group or event against which the government can't offer protection. The threat may come from a rebel group that opposes the government, or a powerful religious group that persecutes others. The government may be afraid of or sympathetic to the group, and so it allows the group to do as it pleases, even if it is committing or threatening to commit violence against innocent citizens.

The third and most important part of the definition is the section about persecution. A refugee must have either experienced persecution firsthand or have a "well-founded fear" of persecu-

For two decades, the United States has accepted African women asylees who face the threat of female genitial mutilation (FGM) in countries like Sudan, Mali, and Egypt.

tion were he or she to return to the home country. It is important to recognize that persecution has as much to do with the victim as the persecutor. Unlike random mistreatment or harm, persecution is more personal in nature: people who are persecuted are singled out for who they are, what they say, or what groups they belong to. The refugee definition lays out five grounds of persecution: race, religion, nationality, membership in a social group, and political opinion. Only persecution under these grounds can qualify people as refugees.

Grounds of Persecution

The first three grounds of persecution are fairly self-explanatory. Racial differences are easy to identify, and minority races often make convenient scapegoats for failed governments. Religious minorities, like ethnic minorities, have been persecuted throughout history. Even powerless majorities—such as the black South Africans during the apartheid era of the 20th century—can be victims of persecution.

Political opinion is often less a result of someone's background than his or her beliefs. Many times individuals will be targeted even though they have done nothing extraordinary except stand as political opponents of a regime or another powerful social group. A new government may persecute people making speeches, handing out leaflets, and even attending a political meeting or rally. Or it may persecute members of a former regime's military. In many cases the persecution extends to officers' families or friends. To be granted asylum, applicants must prove their connection to this persecuted group.

The most difficult to pin down of the five grounds of persecution is "membership in a particular social group." This does not necessarily mean a formally organized group, but simply a class of people with a common characteristic. Cases that follow these criteria are less common but often receive attention in the media. They include women who claim persecution for being Westernized in an Islamic country; gay men or women who have been individually targeted by an oppressive government; or members of a disfavored professional association.

The United States has accepted African women asylees who fall under this category of persecution. Unlike many other asylees, these women did not flee a particular conflict, but an entire culture. In many African countries, including Mali, Sudan, Togo, and Egypt, all women and girls may undergo a procedure in which they are mutilated in the genital area. It is a horrifying, painful, and widespread practice.

The decision to accept refugees who feared genital mutilation presented a legal problem. The people conducting the procedure would argue that it is not meant specifically to punish or harm the women. As terrifying as it is, the traditionalists consider it to be a rite of passage into womanhood. Could this be persecution?

 ### Refugee Resettlement

Refugees differ from asylees in that they are interviewed outside the United States before they are resettled. The interviews are done by immigration personnel, with policy guidance from the U.S. Department of State. Every year, in consultation with Congress, the president sets a ceiling on the number of refugees the United States will admit. For example, President Barack Obama set a ceiling of 70,000 refugees for 2015. Obama determined that the ceiling should be raised to 85,000 in 2016.

There is no cap on the number of people who may be granted asylum in the United States in a given year. However, only 10,000 per year can become lawful permanent residents (allowed to stay permanently). Those who receive asylum but have not received one of these 10,000 slots are permitted to work; however, they do not enjoy other benefits of permanent residence, such as accruing time toward the five years required to be eligible for U.S. citizenship.

A U.S. immigration court case in 1996 stated that it is. Fauziya Kassindja, a teenager from Togo who feared facing genital mutilation if she were forced to return to her home country, was granted asylum.

Asylum in the United States

Kassindja's asylum case is one example of the ongoing debates over what exactly defines persecution. While the Immigration and Nationality Act of 1965 does not define the term, U.S. courts and the United States Bureau of Citizenship and Immigration (USCIS)—formerly the Immigration and Naturalization Service (INS)—have reached a workable definition. Persecution as defined by the courts is "the infliction of suffering or harm on those who differ in a way that is regarded as offensive." Threats to life and freedom—including slavery, torture, and imprisonment without a trial—are always considered persecution. This includes genocide and state-sponsored murder as well. Threats of a lower magnitude, such as discrimination or harassment, are more open to consideration. The level of harm that would constitute persecution is decided by asylum officers and immigration courts. While individual cases vary, officers and judges try to adhere to an established precedent in reaching a decision.

Individuals can apply for asylum in two ways. The first way is an affirmative application. This means that the asylum seeker has come forward of his or her own accord and asked the U.S. government for asylum. This may happen immediately upon arrival in the United States, but more often it happens after the individual has lived in the country for months. With an affirmative application, an asylum seeker will schedule an interview with an asylum officer to decide his or her case.

The second way to apply for asylum is a defensive application, which is conducted when an alien is in the middle of proceedings to be deported (formally removed from the country by U.S. authorities). Receiving asylum will prevent someone from being deported. The standard for getting asylum is the same here as with an affirmative application; however, since the applicant is already going through deportation proceedings, the claim is decided by an immigration judge instead of an asylum officer.

Waves of Asylees

When violence or repression sweeps through a particular country, it's common for asylum seekers from that country to head to the United States in two waves. The first wave typically will consist of people with more resources and more education. Some will already speak English, and most will have left their country for political reasons. Usually more individuals of the first wave are able to prove their claims than those arriving later.

Asylum seekers arriving later usually do not come as prepared. Because fewer of them speak English, they have a harder time adjusting to their new lives. They often receive assistance from the communities carved out by the earlier arrivals.

Asylees and refugees in the United States have attained some security, through both the self-sufficiency of their communities and the institution of permanent immigration laws; however, to a certain extent the status of these groups is affected by changes in public opinion. One of the primary factors affecting American attitudes toward asylum seekers is the state of the economy. When the economy is booming, refugees and asylees tend to be welcomed. But when the economy stagnates and unemployment rises, some Americans start to see asylum seekers as a threat and fear that their jobs will be taken.

Another factor that has influenced American attitudes toward asylum seekers—especially those who are Arab or Muslim—is terrorism. The attacks of September 11, 2001, perpetrated by members of the Islamic extremist group al-Qaeda, constituted the deadliest terrorist incident ever on U.S. soil. In all, about 3,000 people lost their lives. The 19 terrorists who carried out the September 11 attacks were all from Arab countries. None, however, was an asylum seeker; they'd all initially entered the United States on tourist, business, or student visas. More recently, the self-styled Islamic State—popularly known as ISIS—

Asylum seekers with limited resources often must use improvised means of transport, as in the case of these Cubans who braved the Florida Straits in a 1951 Chevrolet truck. Apprehended by the U.S. Coast Guard, the passengers of the makeshift boat were sent back to Cuba.

apparently inspired a December 2015 shooting rampage in San Bernardino, California, in which 14 people were killed. Again, the killers weren't asylum seekers but rather an American Muslim and his Pakistani-born wife.

Nonetheless, some Americans came to believe that as a group, asylum seekers, refugees, and other potential immigrants from the Middle East presented an unacceptably high risk of being terrorists. During the campaign for the Republican Party's 2016 presidential nomination, one candidate, Senator Ted Cruz of Texas, proposed banning Syrian Muslims from entering the United States (parts of Syria were ISIS strongholds). Cruz's rival for the Republican nomination, businessman Donald Trump, called for excluding from the country all Muslims who weren't U.S. citizens. That proposal garnered a surprising degree of support from the American public. A YouGov/Huffington Post poll conducted in March 2016 showed 51 percent of Americans in favor of a total ban on Muslims entering the United States.

In recent years, politicians like Donald Trump, a businessman who ran for president in 2016, have argued for greater restriction of asylum seekers.

Restrictionists and Humanitarians

Generally, public opinion shifts power between two impulses that guide asylum policy. There is the restrictionist camp, which wants to put stricter limits on all immigration. This camp views asylum seekers as a source of problems in the country, and therefore advocates limiting asylum as much as possible.

The humanitarian camp has the opposite perspective and believes that the prosperity of the United States should be used to help people from other countries. While it is clear that assisting everyone is not feasible, this camp favors a more open immigration policy, particularly in regard to victims of human rights abuses.

For a long period in U.S. history, there was a subgroup of thw humanitarian camp with its own perspective on refugee policy. The anti-communists, active during the Cold War—the decades-long struggle for global influence between the United States and the communist Soviet Union, believed that American foreign policy should be dedicated to fighting the spread of communism. Anti-communists used refugee policy to further their agenda. By helping refugees and asylees from communist countries, they argued, Americans were indirectly enfeebling communism while also aiding its victims.

This thinking influenced asylum policy for decades but faded with the end of the Cold War and the collapse of the Soviet Union in 1991. Today, the humanitarian camp seeks to direct its attention on the asylum seekers themselves, although there remains an underlying notion that providing assistance to refugees is an indirect way to combat the persecution committed by unjust governments.

 # Text-Dependent Questions

1. What group of Iranians did Parvaneh Vahidmanesh want to study?
2. What event triggered massive demonstrations in Iran in 2009?
3. Which country was the main adversary of the United States during the Cold War?

 # Research Project

Read about the history of Iran. Then create a timeline of important events in that country since 1900.

2 IMMIGRATION AND ASYLUM POLICY

For over a century, the United States and Canada have used laws to control the flow of immigrants, including asylum seekers. But this was not always the case. North America was founded and built by immigrants, many of whom were escaping persecution much like the refugees of today.

In the 17th and 18th century, many groups who formed the colonies that would become the United States sought asylum, although it wasn't regulated like the present-day asylum system. The Puritans founded Massachusetts as a solution to escape religious persecution in England. Pennsylvania was a safe haven for the English Quakers, as well as German religious groups such as Moravians and Mennonites. Lord Baltimore, founder of Maryland, encouraged fellow Catholics to become colony members so that they could practice their religion without fear of persecution.

To better understand how asylum and asylees fit into the U.S. and Canadian immigration systems, it is helpful to take a look at the history of immigration in both countries.

A Short History of U.S. Immigration

Immigration to the United States has been characterized by openness punctuated by periods of restriction. During the 17th,

◀ Immigrants wait to pass through customs at New York City's Ellis Island, 1905. Asylees join the millions of immigrants who move to North America for reasons other than to escape persecution.

18th, and 19th centuries, immigration was essentially open without restriction, and, at times, immigrants were even recruited to come to America. Between 1783 and 1820, approximately 250,000 immigrants arrived at U.S. shores. Between 1841 and 1860, more than 4 million immigrants came; most were from England, Ireland, and Germany.

Historically, race and ethnicity have played a role in legislation to restrict immigration. The Chinese Exclusion Act of 1882, which was not repealed until 1943, specifically prevented Chinese people from becoming U.S. citizens and did not allow Chinese laborers to immigrate for the next decade. An agreement with Japan in the early 1900s prevented most Japanese immigration to the United States.

Until the 1920s, no numerical restrictions on immigration existed in the United States, although health restrictions applied. The only other significant restrictions came in 1917, when passing a literacy test became a requirement for immigrants. Presidents Cleveland, Taft, and Wilson had vetoed similar measures earlier. In addition, in 1917 a prohibition was added to the law against the immigration of people from Asia (defined as the Asiatic barred zone). While a few of these prohibitions were lifted during World War II, they were not repealed until 1952, and even then Asians were only allowed in under very small annual quotas.

 Words to Understand in This Chapter

capitalism—an economic system that permits the ownership of private property and allows individuals and companies to compete for their own economic gain.

Holocaust—the mass killing of Jews by Nazi Germany during World War II.

parole—a process by which people who don't meet the requirements for receiving a visa may be admitted temporarily into the United States, generally for humanitarian reasons.

Immigration Policy from World War I to 1965

During World War I, the federal government required that all travelers to the United States obtain a visa at a U.S. consulate or diplomatic post abroad. As former State Department consular affairs officer C. D. Scully points out, by making that requirement permanent Congress, by 1924, established the framework of temporary, or non-immigrant visas (for study, work, or travel), and immigrant visas (for permanent residence). That framework remains in place today.

After World War I, cultural intolerance and bizarre racial theories led to new immigration restrictions. The House Judiciary Committee employed a eugenics consultant, Dr. Harry N. Laughlin, who asserted that certain races were inferior. Another leader of the eugenics movement, Madison Grant, argued that Jews, Italians, and others were inferior because of their supposedly different skull size.

The Immigration Act of 1924, preceded by the Temporary Quota Act of 1921, set new numerical limits on immigration based on "national origin." Taking effect in 1929, the 1924 act set annual quotas on immigrants that were specifically designed to keep out southern Europeans, such as Italians and Greeks. Generally no more than 100 people of the proscribed nationalities were permitted to immigrate.

While the new law was rigid, the U.S. Department of State's restrictive interpretation directed consular officers overseas to be even stricter in their application of the "public charge" provision. (A public charge is someone unable to support himself or his family.) As author Laura Fermi wrote, "In response to the new cry for restriction at the beginning of the [Great Depression] . . . the consuls were to interpret very strictly the clause prohibiting admission of aliens 'likely to become public charges; and to deny the visa to an applicant who in their opinion might become a public charge at any time.'"

In the early 1900s, more than one million immigrants a year came to the United States. In 1930—the first year of the national-origin quotas—approximately 241,700 immigrants were admitted. But under the State Department's strict interpretations, only 23,068 immigrants entered during 1933, the smallest total since 1831. Later these restrictions prevented many Jews in Germany and elsewhere in Europe from escaping what would become the Holocaust. At the height of the Holocaust in 1943, the United States admitted fewer than 6,000 refugees.

The Displaced Persons Act of 1948, the nation's first refugee law, allowed many refugees from World War II to settle in the United States. The law put into place policy changes that had already seen immigration rise from 38,119 in 1945 to 108,721 in 1946 (and later to 249,187 in 1950). One-third of those admitted between 1948 and 1951 were Poles, with ethnic Germans forming the second-largest group.

The 1952 Immigration and Nationality Act is best known for its restrictions against those who supported communism or anarchy. However, the bill's other provisions were quite restrictive and were passed over the veto of President Truman. The 1952 act retained the national-origin quota system for the Eastern Hemisphere. The Western Hemisphere continued to operate without a quota and relied on other qualitative factors to limit immigration. Moreover, during that time, the Mexican bracero program, from 1942 to 1964, allowed millions of Mexican agricultural workers to work temporarily in the United States.

The 1952 act set aside half of each national quota to be divided among three preference categories for relatives of U.S. citizens and permanent residents. The other half went to aliens with high education or exceptional abilities. These quotas applied only to those from the Eastern Hemisphere.

A Halt to the National-Origin Quotas

The Immigration and Nationality Act of 1965 became a landmark in immigration legislation by specifically striking the racially based national-origin quotas. It removed the barriers to Asian immigration, which later led to opportunities to immigrate for many Filipinos, Chinese, Koreans, and others. The Western Hemisphere was designated a ceiling of 120,000 immigrants but

President Lyndon Johnson signed the Immigration Act of 1965, inaugurating a new era of immigration. With the passage of the act, many foreign groups were able to immigrate to the United States in large numbers.

without a preference system or per country limits. Modifications made in 1978 ultimately combined the Western and Eastern Hemispheres into one preference system and one ceiling of 290,000.

The 1965 act built on the existing system—without the national-origin quotas—and gave somewhat more priority to family relationships. It did not completely overturn the existing system but rather carried forward essentially intact the family immigration categories from the 1959 amendments to the Immigration and Nationality Act. Even though the text of the law prior to 1965 indicated that half of the immigration slots were reserved for skilled employment immigration, in practice, Immigration and Naturalization Service (INS) statistics show that 86 percent of the visas issued between 1952 and 1965 went for family immigration.

A number of significant pieces of legislation since 1980 have shaped the current U.S. immigration system. First, the Refugee Act of 1980 removed refugees from the annual world limit and established that the president would set the number of refugees who could be admitted each year after consultations with Congress.

Second, the 1986 Immigration Reform and Control Act (IRCA) introduced sanctions against employers who "knowingly" hired undocumented immigrants (those here illegally). It also provided amnesty for many undocumented immigrants.

Third, the Immigration Act of 1990 increased legal immigration by 40 percent. In particular, the act significantly increased the number of employment-based immigrants (to 140,000), while also boosting family immigration.

Fourth, the 1996 Illegal Immigration Reform and Immigrant Responsibility Act (IIRAIRA) significantly tightened rules that permitted undocumented immigrants to convert to legal status and made other changes that tightened immigration law in areas such as political asylum and deportation.

Fifth, in response to the September 11, 2001, terrorist attacks, the USA PATRIOT Act and the Enhanced Border Security and Visa Entry Reform Act tightened rules on the granting of visas to individuals from certain countries and enhanced the federal government's monitoring and detention authority over foreign nationals in the United States.

In a dramatic reorganization of the federal government, the Homeland Security Act of 2002 abolished the Immigration and Naturalization Service and transferred its immigration service and enforcement functions from the Department of Justice into a new Department of Homeland Security. The Customs Service, the Coast Guard, and parts of other agencies were also transferred into the new department.

A Short History of Canadian Immigration

In the 1800s, immigration into Canada was largely unrestricted. Farmers and artisans from England and Ireland made up a significant portion of 19th-century immigrants. England's

Parliament passed laws that facilitated and encouraged the voyage to North America, particularly for the poor.

After the United States barred Chinese railroad workers from settling in the country, Canada encouraged the immigration of Chinese laborers to assist in the building of Canadian railways. Responding to the racial views of the time, the Canadian Parliament began charging a "head tax" for Chinese and South Asian (Indian) immigrants in 1885. The fee of $50—later raised to $500—was well beyond the means of laborers making one or two dollars a day. Later, the government sought additional ways to prohibit Asians from entering the country. For example, it decided to require a "continuous journey," meaning that immigrants to Canada had to travel from their country on a boat that made an uninterrupted passage. For immigrants or asylum seekers from Asia this was nearly impossible.

As the 20th century progressed, concerns about race led to further restrictions on immigration to Canada. These restrictions particularly hurt Jewish and other refugees seeking to flee persecution in Europe. Government statistics indicate that Canada accepted no more than 5,000 Jewish refugees before and during the Holocaust.

After World War II, Canada, like the United States, began accepting thousands of Europeans displaced by the war. Canada's laws were modified to accept these war refugees, as well as Hungarians fleeing Communist authorities after the crushing of the 1956 Hungarian Revolution.

The Immigration Act of 1952 in Canada allowed for a "tap on, tap off" approach to immigration, granting administrative authorities the power to allow more immigrants into the country in good economic times, and fewer in times of recession. The shortcoming of such an approach is that there is little evidence immigrants harm a national economy and much evidence they contribute to economic growth, particularly in the growth of the labor force.

In 1966 the government of Prime Minister Lester Pearson introduced a policy statement stressing how immigrants were key to Canada's economic growth. With Canada's relatively small population base, it became clear that in the absence of newcomers, the country would not be able to grow. The policy was introduced four years after Parliament enacted important legislation that eliminated Canada's own version of racially based national-origin quotas.

In 1967 a new law established a points system that awarded entry to potential immigrants using criteria based primarily on an individual's age, language ability, skills, education, family relationships, and job prospects. The total points needed for entry of an immigrant is set by the Minister of Citizenship and Immigration Canada. The new law also established a category for humanitarian (refugee) entry.

The 1976 Immigration Act refined and expanded the possibility for entry under the points system, particularly for those seeking to sponsor family members. The act also expanded refugee and asylum law to comport with Canada's international obligations. The law established five basic categories for immigration into Canada: 1) family; 2) humanitarian; 3) independents (including skilled workers), who immigrate to Canada on their own; 4) assisted relatives; and 5) business immigrants (including investors, entrepreneurs, and the self-employed).

The new Immigration and Refugee Protection Act, which took effect June 28, 2002, made a series of modifications to existing Canadian immigration law. The act, and the regulations that followed, toughened rules on those seeking asylum and the process for removing people unlawfully in Canada.

The law modified the points system, adding greater flexibility for skilled immigrants and temporary workers to become permanent residents, and evaluating skilled workers on the weight of their transferable skills as well as those of their specific occupation. The legislation also made it easier for employers to have a labor shortage declared in an industry or sector, which would facilitate the entry of foreign workers in that industry or sector.

On family immigration, the act permitted parents to sponsor dependent children up to the age of 22 (previously 19 was the

The ocean liner *St. Louis*, carrying 937 German Jewish refugees, was refused permission to dock in Miami in May 1939. It was forced to return its passengers to Europe, where they faced Nazi persecution.

maximum age at which a child could be sponsored for immigration). The act also allowed partners in common-law arrangements, including same-sex partners, to be considered as family members for the purpose of immigration sponsorship. Along with these liberalizing measures, the act also included provisions to address perceived gaps in immigration-law enforcement.

U.S. Asylum Policy

In the years leading up to World War II (1939-1945), the atmosphere in the United States and Canada toward immigrants and asylum seekers was not welcoming. The period was marked by a depressed economy, restrictive laws, and negative stereotypes of foreigners, all of which contributed to a sense of inhospitality.

Perhaps the incident that most famously reflected this sentiment was the rejection of refugees aboard an ocean liner known as the *St. Louis*. In May 1939, the *St. Louis* sailed from

Hamburg, Germany. It carried 937 passengers, most of whom were Jews fleeing the Nazi regime in Germany. They had filed for U.S. visas and had secured Cuban transit visas, which would allow them to stay in Cuba while the U.S. visas were being processed. However, when the ship reached Havana, Cuban authorities refused to let the passengers disembark, and after a few days, the transit visas were canceled.

The *St. Louis* left Havana and tried to dock in Miami. The U.S. government refused to allow the ship into port, however. A group of Canadian church leaders appealed to Prime Minister William Lyon Mackenzie King to accept the refugees. But the prime minister refused.

With no alternatives, the *St. Louis* sailed back to Europe with all passengers still on board. Fortunately, England, France, Belgium, and the Netherlands agreed to take in Jewish refugees from the ship. But after Nazi armies overran continental Europe during World War II, more than 250 of the people who'd set sail on the St. Louis lost their lives in the Holocaust.

After the war, changes to U.S. law finally made allowances for refugees. With the passing of the Displaced Persons Act of 1948, 205,000 refugees were permitted to enter the United States over the next two years. Groups that came in over their designated quota would have slots taken out of the quotas for future years. The act was the first step toward legally recognizing asylum seekers.

United Nations High Commissioner for Refugees

The world's leading countries took the next step in 1950, establishing the United Nations High Commissioner for Refugees (UNHCR). UNHCR was put in place to find international solutions to refugee problems. In 1951, it directed its attention exclusively to the 400,000 refugees in Europe. Its budget was $300,000, and it had a staff of 33 people.

After more than 65 years in existence, UNCHR has grown dramatically. By 2015 its staff had increased to more than 9,300,

Filippo Grandi took office as UN High Commissioner for Refugees in 2016.

and they operated in nearly 125 countries across the globe. The $300,000 budget had grown to $7 billion. Its mission has extended beyond helping refugees; now asylees, internally displaced people, returnees, and war-affected populations also receive assistance. In 2015, UNHCR provided protection and assistance to almost 55 million people in crisis.

UNHCR's first action was adopting the 1951 Convention Relating to the Status of Refugees. This treaty defined the term *refugee*. It also set down refugee rights, including that of non-refoulement. All those deemed refugees have the right to remain outside of their homeland. Countries who signed the Convention promised to honor those rights.

The United States did not sign the 1951 Convention, but it did sign the 1967 Protocol Relating to the Status of Refugees, which incorporates the terms of the Convention. Instead of following the course of action of most UN member countries, the United States developed its own way of dealing with refugees, which was informed greatly by Cold War policy. Soon after the Second World War, relations between the U.S. and the Soviet Union cooled, due in large part to Soviet domination of Eastern European countries. The Cold War pitted America's liberal democracy and capitalism against the Soviet Union's communism. Although the two superpower adversaries spent huge sums of money and committed vast resources to preparing for a military confrontation, they never fought each other directly. In an effort to secure allies they did, however, support opposing sides in various civil wars and regional conflicts.

By the middle of the 1950s, the cold war agenda had worked

its way into U.S. immigration policy. In 1955, the National Security Council of the Eisenhower administration issued a memorandum to fight international communism. The memo endorsed a variety of covert activities, including providing assistance to "refugee liberation groups." Any enemy of communism was thereafter deemed a friend of the United States.

Paroling Refugees

In October 1956, a popular revolt in Hungary temporarily ousted the communist regime. The Soviets responded by sending tanks and troops into the country to suppress the uprising. Tens of thousands of Hungarian refugees fled to Austria and Yugoslavia for safety.

Seeking to help the refugees, the U.S. attorney general used the authority to "parole" aliens into the United States. This procedure allowed people to enter the country but did not give them

Soviet tanks station at strategic points of an intersection in Budapest, Hungary, to thwart the popular uprising of October 1956. In the wake of the Soviet invasion, the U.S. Attorney General authorized the entry of 32,000 Hungarians uprooted by the conflict.

the right to stay permanently. Attorney General Herbert Brownell Jr. brought in 32,000 Hungarians this way, and established a precedent for handling refugee crises that lasted until 1980.

Although Congress didn't control the flow of refugees, it could make decisions on their status once they arrived. For example, in 1958 Hungarians were given the option to pursue permanent resident status. The next step for these lawful residents, if they wanted to take it, was to apply for citizenship.

Although the Immigration Act of 1965 opened up immigration to other ethnic groups, there were still a limited number of visas that were offered each year. Under the 1965 law, refugees would be accepted if they were fleeing communist countries, or fleeing from the Middle East and had a fear of persecution based on race, religion, or political opinion. Also, the law allowed the acceptance of victims of a "catastrophic natural calamity" (such as an earthquake), though the president would have the discretion to determine which natural disasters met the threshold for being truly catastrophic. Legislators believed that it was likely the clauses of the law could handle future refugee admissions, but the refugee crises during the second half of the 20th century would prove them wrong.

 # Text-Dependent Questions

1. Name at least two groups that moved to North America in the 17th or 18th century in order to escape religious discrimination in Europe.

2. When it left Hamburg, Germany, in May 1939, to which country did the St. Louis first sail?

3. In what year was the United Nations High Commissioner for Refugees (UNHCR) established?

 # Research Project

Using a library or the Internet, find out more about the Hungarian revolution of 1956. Write a one-page report that details the causes of the uprising and the consequences.

3 BOATLIFTS FROM THE CARIBBEAN

When the Eisenhower administration paroled the Hungarians fleeing the Soviet invasion in November 1956, a parole system for refugee admissions was set in motion. The system further meshed refugee admissions into the framework of U.S. foreign policy, and began a legacy that lasted decades and affected hundreds of thousands of lives.

During the 1950s, U.S. foreign policy was staunchly anti-communist. The refugee and asylum decisions made during that period—in particular the long-standing resolution to shelter Cuban exiles—reflect this stance.

In 1959, Fidel Castro overthrew Cuba's dictator, General Fulgencio Batista. After cementing his power, Castro surrounded himself with hard-line communists. He nationalized U.S. businesses operating in Cuba, banned political parties, and shut down labor groups. Soon he controlled hospitals, newspapers, and radio stations. Step by step, Castro took control of everything. Those who opposed him were interrogated, imprisoned, or worse.

The First Exiles

Soon after Castro's revolution, Cubans began to leave the coun-

◀Cuban president Fidel Castro announces victory in the revolution to oust dictator Fulgencio Batista, January 1959. As a form of opposition to Castro's communist regime, instituted shortly after the revolution, the U.S. immigration system has provided asylum to Cuban exiles for over five decades.

try. Members of Batista's government left the island first. Next to go were upper- and middle-class professionals and their families. Many left for Spain or Latin America; others went to the United States, with which they generally were familiar. Many had traveled to the United States before or had friends or contacts living there.

On the whole this first group of Cuban exiles was older and better educated than most immigrant groups. It was also wealthier, and the exiles initially were able to bring substantial assets to the United States. Soon, however, Castro ordered the confiscation of the property and money of departing Cubans, who were allowed to carry no more than five dollars in their pockets when they left the country. By 1961, Cubans entering the United States arrived with almost nothing.

Cuba kept the exiles' money, but it lost a vast resource of talented people with plenty of initiative. Between January 1959 and April 1961, 125,000 Cubans entered the United States. Included in this group were the children of Operation Pedro Pan. Initiated by an American nonprofit organization in 1960, Operation Pedro Pan secured visas for unaccompanied Cuban children, and by 1962 had brought more than 14,000 children to the United States.

Although the United States planned to resettle Cuban exiles throughout the country, most settled in Miami, where there was a rapidly growing Cuban population. Eventually, Miami's "Little Havana" community also drew Cuban exiles living in Spain and Latin America.

For the refugees, the older individuals in particular, change

 Words to Understand in This Chapter

interdiction—the act of intercepting and preventing the further movement of people or goods.

legacy—something received from the past.

nationalize—to transfer (a business or industry) from private ownership to government control.

was difficult. Because their manners were Cuban and they spoke a different language, many took jobs that required very little English. A number of the refugees were overqualified for their work—business managers, engineers, and doctors became taxi drivers and short-order cooks. They hoped that they would live under these difficult circumstances for only a short period. Few people thought that the United States would allow a communist government to operate so close to its borders, and many believed Cuba would soon be liberated. Until that happened, the exiles planned to stay in Miami, where the climate was similar and the homeland was just a short plane flight away.

A Failed Invasion

In March 1960, the U.S. Central Intelligence Agency (CIA) began training a force of Cuban exiles to invade Cuba and overthrow Castro's regime. Shortly before midnight on April 16, 1961, the exiles began landing in southern Cuba at a place called the Bay of Pigs. But the invaders encountered unexpectedly strong resistance, and by April 19 they'd been defeated.

The Cuban exiles' hopes for a quick return to their country suffered a huge blow as a result of the Bay of Pigs fiasco. The events of October 1962 nearly killed those hopes completely. During that month American spy planes detected missile silos in Cuba, where nuclear missiles had arrived from the Soviet Union. President John F. Kennedy ordered the U.S. Navy to form a ring around Cuba, preventing any ships from carrying missile components or other offensive weapons from reaching the island. The world appeared to be on the brink of nuclear war, with Cuba at the center.

After several tense days, the Soviets and the United States worked out a compromise. The Soviets promised to dismantle the nuclear missile sites in Cuba, and the United States promised to stop supporting efforts to overthrow Castro. All flights to the United States from Cuba were canceled. The Castro government forbade citizens to leave the island. Nonetheless, tens of thousands of Cubans tried to escape the communist regime by sea. They piled

President John F. Kennedy signs Proclamation 3504, authorizing a U.S. Navy quarantine of Cuba, in October 1962. The blockade was intended to keep Soviet ships carrying military supplies from reaching the island.

aboard small, often rickety boats or constructed their own rafts made from materials such as tire inner tubes and attempted to cross the Straits of Florida to reach the United States. Some were caught by the Cuban authorities and received long prison sentences. Others drowned or died from dehydration on the perilous journey. But between 1962 and 1965, an estimated 30,000 Cubans successfully sailed from Cuba to Florida.

The situation in Cuba changed abruptly in 1965. Discontent had built up to such a level that Castro decided he had to give potential defectors the opportunity to leave. Without warning, he announced that he was allowing Cubans to emigrate. Anyone who had family in the United States could get a visa to leave Cuba, and he invited Cubans living in the United States to pick up their family members at Camarioca harbor. Thousands of small boats made the trip. Over 5,000 migrants arrived in the United States before the INS stopped the boatlift.

The sudden departure of so many migrants resulted in chaos. Cubans demanded a more organized emigration procedure, and as a result, direct plane flights from Cuba were resumed. People would regularly fly from Havana to the United States aboard U.S.-chartered planes on what were called "Freedom Flights." The new plan would be legal and orderly.

In the 1960s and 1970s, the attorney general's authority to parole people into the United States gave Cubans the permission to stay lawfully in the country. However, their status as permanent residents (green card holders) was not guaranteed. The Cuban Adjustment Act, passed in 1966, was a crucial piece of legislation that addressed this issue, and over the decades it would guide much of U.S. policy towards Cuban refugees. The law allowed Cubans to become green card holders after being physically present in the United States for two years (later reduced to one year) or more, regardless of how they first arrived. Between 1966 and 2013, more than a million Cubans have been granted permanent resident status, according to the Office of Immigration Statistics.

Cuba and the 1980 Refugee Act

During the decades that large waves of Cuban refugees arrived and were resettled, the United States was gradually expanding on its definition of a refugee. The United Nations had encouraged world leaders to broaden their perspective on the issue. The 1967 Protocol Relating to the Status of Refugees made slight changes to the refugee definition, removing it from the specific context of World War II and expanding its application beyond Europe to the rest of the world.

As presidential administrations changed, so did asylum policy. In 1979 President Jimmy Carter formed the Office of the U.S. Coordinator for Refugee Affairs, and the following year in March he signed the Refugee Act of 1980. Thereafter, the way in which the United States handled refugees and asylees was fundamentally different.

First, the act redefined the term *refugee*. Before it was passed, there was one important difference between the American definition and the UN definition. The older American definition specified that refugees were fleeing communist countries or countries in the Middle East, but the Refugee Act removed that language.

The act also enabled the setting of an annual refugee ceiling, which was viewed as a more efficient mechanism than parole. The first ceiling was set at 50,000 refugees for the next two years, and higher ceilings were set in following years. The law also made refugees eligible for certain social programs and allowed them to apply for permanent resident status after living one year in the country.

Yet another change instituted by the Refugee Act had immediate consequences. Asylum was now recognized as separate from the refugee system. Any foreign national in the United States—whether that person arrived legally or not—could

A boat full of Cuban refugees arrives in Key West, Florida, as part of the massive Mariel boatlift of 1980, which entailed the sudden influx of more than 125,000 refugees. After the Refugee Act of 1980 was passed, these refugees were protected from deportation.

request asylum. And if judged to have a legitimate fear of persecution in his or her country of origin, the person would be able to remain in the United States. What's more, the Refugee Act made asylees eligible for the same benefits as refugees, including cash assistance, health care, and education.

The Boatlifts of 1980

The new asylum legislation had immediate consequences for Cuban exiles. and with Cuba's economy foundering, Fidel Castro suddenly announced that Cubans who wished to leave the island would be permitted to do so. They'd have to depart from the port of Mariel, and they'd need to have their own boat transportation.

In response to Castro's announcement, Cuban exiles in Florida began chartering boats and heading to Mariel to pick up family members and friends. President Carter initially announced that the United States would admit 3,500 Cubans as refugees. But the number of people being ferried out of Mariel quickly exceeded that figure. The Straits of Florida teemed with crowded boats, some of them barely seaworthy.

At the height of what became known as the Mariel boatlift, the Coast Guard picked up 5,000 Cubans each day. Nearly 125,000 Cubans applied for asylum after reaching the United States.

In May, an average of nearly 2,800 Cubans arrived every day, overwhelming the available resources in South Florida. Assessing the magnitude of the situation, President Carter decided to put the new asylum privileges on hold and instead assign the recently arrived Cubans a special entrant status. They were not granted automatic asylum, but they were protected from deportation until their status was resolved. The procedure was the equivalent of parole, even though the new law officially ended that process.

Despite Carter's decision to suspend certain asylum privileges, a large percentage of the Cubans fleeing in 1980 were eventually granted asylum. In contrast, Haitians fleeing their country at the time—estimated to number more than 5,000—

were treated quite differently. Many didn't make it to the United States at all.

U.S. Asylum Policy and Haiti

During the Cold War, American policy makers were willing to support right-wing dictators if they deemed that necessary to prevent the spread of communism. One such dictator was François Duvalier, who ruled Haiti with an iron fist from 1957 to 1971. During those years, Haiti maintained pro-Western policies, but government corruption was rampant, and Haiti's people suffered from widespread poverty and a range of human-rights abuses. Haitians had no genuine political freedom. Opposition political leaders, activists, and journalists faced arrest or government-sanctioned violence.

In spite of Duvalier's brutality and repression, the United States maintained close ties with the regime, which was reliably anti-communist. As a result, American policy makers downplayed the persecution Haitians faced. People who fled Haiti tended not to be seen as true refugees.

When François Duvalier died in 1971, his son Jean-Claude took over. In many ways the younger Duvalier was even more repressive than his father. By 1972, a Haitian exodus was in motion. Over the next eight years, approximately 30,000 Haitians entered the United States by boat. Thousands of them sought asylum, but fewer than 100 were approved.

Unlike Cubans, Haitians picked up at sea by the Coast Guard were considered "excludable." Until 1974, they were returned to Haiti without a hearing. In 1975, an American organization known as the National Council of Churches (NCC) sued the

President François "Papa Doc" Duvalier (1907–71) ushered in an era of government repression in Haiti that continued with his son, Jean-Claude ("Baby Doc"), the country's president from 1971 to 1986. Although many Haitians were victims of persecution during the Duvalier era, the United States only granted asylum to a limited number of Haitians.

INS, claiming that it had treated Haitian refugees unfairly and was following a double standard. The NCC invoked the 1967 Protocol, which had become the bill of rights for refugees, and argued that by returning Haitians to Haiti, the United States was violating refugees' rights. The churches' case was denied, but other cases were filed in its wake.

Organizations advocating for the Haitians were encouraged by the passage of the 1980 Refugee Act. With the anti-communist language removed from the U.S. definition of refugees, Haitian

 The Asylum Corps and Temporary Protected Status

The asylum system was modified during the administration of George H. W. Bush. In 1990, final regulations were added to the Refugee Act of 1980 that separated asylum procedures from other INS matters. Legislators had acted in the hope that the asylum process would be less influenced by political agendas. The INS established an "Asylum Corps" of specially trained officers who would exclusively work on asylum cases. (Today, responsibility for affirmative asylum cases lies with the Asylum Division of U.S. Citizenship and Immigration Services.) These officers began keeping files on countries of origin, making it easier to gather information on applicants' backgrounds.

The new regulations also set a limit of 90 days to process an asylum request. If an applicant did not have an interview by then, he or she would be granted a work permit until the case was decided. However, a combination of factors led to a staggering backlog of asylum cases. The understaffed Asylum Corps labored to keep pace, and the process was further complicated by false asylum claims to get work permits.

Finally, the 1990 regulations brought into existence "Temporary Protected Status," or TPS. It continues to exist as part of the U.S. asylum system. As long as asylum seekers have TPS, they may find work and stay in the United States without fear of deportation. The secretary of the Department of Homeland Security may designate a country for TPS because of a civil war or other ongoing armed conflict; because of a natural disaster (such as a hurricane or an earthquake) or a disease epidemic; or because of some other dire but temporary situation. After a TPS designation is made, individuals from the country in question who are in the United States may apply for TPS. Upon approval, they receive the right to live and work in the United States until their country's TPS designation is removed. TPS doesn't make a person eligible for permanent residency or change his or her immigration status in any other way.

Thirteen countries were designated for TPS as of early 2016. Those countries were: El Salvador, Guinea, Haiti, Honduras, Liberia, Nepal, Nicaragua, Sierra Leone, Somalia, Sudan, South Sudan, Syria, and Yemen.

applicants could now at least be considered for the same status that individuals from communist countries received. In July 1980, a federal district judge acknowledged that a double standard was being used, and he halted the deportation of more than 4,000 Haitians. He ruled that their cases were not heard with the same care that the cases of Cubans received. He also accused the INS of acting on a bias, and ordered that the courts hear another round of individual cases.

Like Cubans, Haitians at this stage were now protected from deportation until they received a fair hearing. Haitian and Cuban hearings would continue to take place, and in accordance with the policy, both groups would receive equal treatment.

A New Policy of Interdiction

After President Ronald Reagan took office in 1981, his administration sought to stop the asylum cases at their source. He issued an executive order to the Coast Guard to intercept Haitian boats and tow them back to Port-au-Prince, Haiti. This procedure was called interdiction. Those Haitians who made it past the Coast Guard were now placed in guarded camps. They were held without bail, and were almost always deported afterward. From a restrictionist standpoint, Reagan's policy was effective. Very few Haitians made it to the United States in 1981; the year before, 12,000 Haitians had arrived.

The Reagan administration's interdiction policy was by no means popular with everyone. Amnesty International, a human rights organization, testified that Haitian refugees were in real danger if they returned to Haiti. The United Nations High Commissioner for Refugees opposed interdiction as well, arguing that Haitians were not being given a fair hearing. The Reagan administration's response was that hearings were being conducted at sea aboard Coast Guard ships. With or without hearings, however, the results were still the same: according to the Congressional Research Service, 22,940 Haitians were intercepted at sea between 1981 and 1990, with only 11 allowed to apply for asylum by the U.S. government.

Some who opposed the administration's policy claimed that interdiction was no less severe than Thailand's refusal of thousands of Vietnamese refugees during that time. After the Vietnam War, South Vietnamese refugees took to the sea to escape the recently installed communist government. The "boat people," as they were called, were kept from ports of the region. In Thailand, they were pushed away, often at gunpoint, by the country's armed forces. Many Vietnamese died at sea from starvation, exposure, and drowning.

Despite the similarities observed by human rights groups between the American policy of interdiction and the Thai government's refusal of the refugees, there were significant differences. The U.S. Coast Guard was safely towing boats back to port, not pushing them out to sea. Also, the Reagan administration interpreted the 1967 Protocol to apply only to areas within U.S. borders. Because interdiction took place on international waters, it was technically not refoulement. Although UNHCR and other organizations contested this defense, the U.S. Supreme Court ultimately upheld the Reagan administration's stance.

The political situation in Haiti temporarily improved when the country's first democratically elected president, Jean-Bertrand Aristide, took office in February 1991. President George H. W. Bush ended the U.S. policy of interdicting Haitians at sea. In late September of 1991, however, Aristide was ousted in a military coup. Amid a spasm of renewed political violence, Haitians again began leaving their country in droves, and President Bush ordered the U.S. Coast Guard to resume interdictions.

By spring of 1992 the Coast Guard had intercepted 38,000 Haitians since Aristide was forced from power. Many were brought to the U.S. naval base at Guantánamo Bay, Cuba, and more than 10,400 were paroled into the United States after they were screened and found to have a credible fear of persecution. The parole gave them at least an opportunity to gain asylum through a complete interview with the INS.

However, in May 1992 President Bush ordered the Coast

Haitians take to the streets of Port-au-Prince to celebrate the election of Jean-Paul Aristide in December 1990.

Guard to intercept all Haitians in boats and immediately return them without interviews. This was a controversial decision that human rights organizations considered a violation of international law. In July the United States Second Circuit Court of Appeals ruled against the Bush administration's policy of denying individual Haitians a screening for refugee status. However, the Supreme Court did not uphold the ruling.

Refugee Interviews at Sea

In 1994, the United States began testing a new way to handle refugees from Haiti, which was still in a state of upheaval following the overthrow of President Aristide in 1991. The U.S. government set up a refugee application center on board the hospital ship USNS *Comfort*. Many asylum claims were processed in this manner. However, soon there was an overload of applicants, and the United States decided to put a halt to processing aboard the ship. New migrants were instead held at the U.S. base at Guantánamo Bay. If they were found to be in danger, they could stay in the base's cramped but safe camp; otherwise, they would be taken back to Haiti. That October, the United States helped restore President Aristide to power, and most people returned to Haiti soon afterward.

Around this time, there was a new wave of Cuban migration. It was attributable mostly to a downturn in Cuba's economy. President Bill Clinton responded by expanding interdiction to include Cubans attempting to reach the United States by sea, a practice that continues to this day. In September 1994 the United States and Cuba reached a compromise on the refugee issue. The United States agreed it would take Cubans interdicted at sea to a "safe haven" outside U.S. territory rather than processing them on the mainland as had been done before. The U.S. government also agreed to admit into the United States—through legal channels—a minimum of 20,000 Cuban immigrants a year in addition to the immediate relatives of Cubans who had become U.S. citizens.

In 1995, a significant revision was made to the Cuban Adjustment Act. In what came to be known as the "wet foot, dry foot" policy, Cuban migrants who were interdicted at sea would no longer benefit from the presumption that they were fleeing persecution. They would have to demonstrate an individual fear of persecution, and those who couldn't do so would be sent back to Cuba. However, Cubans who made it to U.S. soil would continue to qualify automatically for political asylum and would receive all the attendant benefits, including a fast track to permanent resident status. The wet foot, dry foot policy led to some bizarre outcomes—including the spectacle of Coast Guard personnel wrestling with Cubans in shallow water off Florida beaches.

Asylum policy regarding Haitians remained controversial during the administration of George W. Bush, who took office in 2001. At the end of that year, the U.S. government started to detain almost all Haitians who made it to U.S. soil via boat.

Attorney General John Ashcroft argued that the policy was necessary to prevent a "mass migration" and, in the spring of 2003, invoked "national security" to justify the continuing detention of the Haitians.

In 2011, Haiti was designated for Temporary Protected Status, so undocumented Haitians in the United States cannot be sent home against their will, unless they've committed a criminal act. TPS for Haiti was set to expire in July 2017, though it could be extended at that time.

Meanwhile, a small but growing chorus of American legislators called for an end to the special treatment of Cuban migrants. This followed efforts by President Barack Obama to normalize U.S. relations with Cuba. Those efforts led, in July 2015, to the restoration of full diplomatic relations between the United States and Cuba—relations that had been severed in 1961. Though Cuba's government remained communist and

Haitian refugees are interdicted at sea and brought aboard a U.S. Coast Guard ship in 1991. After a brief seven-month period of stability during that year, which began with the democratic election of President Jean-Bertrand Aristide, a coup in September spurred another wave of refugees to leave the country.

authoritarian, American policy makers increasingly acknowledged that Cuban migration to the United States was now driven mostly by the desire for improved economic circumstances rather than by political persecution. In March 2016, two congressmen from Texas, Democrat Henry Cuellar and Republican Blake Farenthold, introduced legislation that would repeal the Cuban Adjustment Act. "It is the sense of Congress," their bill stated, "that Cuban nationals should be treated under the same immigration rules as nationals of other countries."

 ## Text-Dependent Questions

1. Where is the Bay of Pigs? What infamous event took place there in 1961?
2. Name the 1966 U.S. law that conferred special status on Cuban migrants.
3. Why did the United States support Haitian dictator François Duvalier?

 ## Research Project

Between December 1960 and October 1962, more than 14,000 unaccompanied Cuban children and youth arrived in Miami as part of what would become known as Operation Pedro Pan. Investigate this extraordinary undertaking, and see if you can find the personal stories of some Pedro Pan children. What do you think it would be like to move to a new country without your parents? If you'd been living in Cuba during the early 1960s, would you have wanted to come to the United States under Operation Pedro Pan? Detail your thoughts in a brief essay.

4 CENTRAL AMERICA

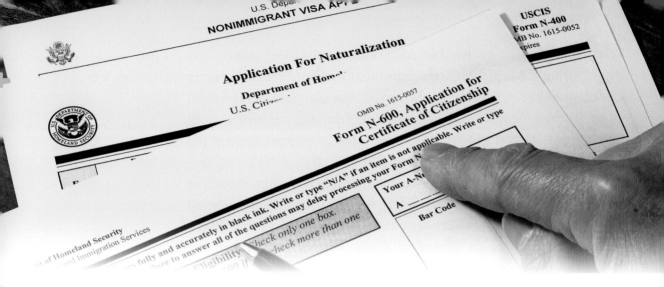

During the 1980s, Central America was engulfed by civil wars and sickening political violence. More than 2 million people from Nicaragua, El Salvador, and Guatemala fled their countries to escape the danger. Many of them made their way north, through Mexico, and entered the United States without proper documents. Of the people who crossed the U.S. border illegally, some promptly requested asylum; others waited until they were more ready. Still others claimed it only as a defense against deportation.

Nicaragua

For more than four decades, one family ruled Nicaragua dictatorially, either directly (by occupying the office of president) or indirectly (through puppet rulers). In 1936, General Anastasio Somoza García—the head of Nicaragua's army, the Guardia Nacional (National Guard)—deposed the country's elected president. Somoza then engineered his own election to the presidency in a ridiculously fraudulent process: the official tally had him receiving more than 107,000 votes, and his opponent just 100. Somoza remained in control until his assassination in 1956, whereupon his son Luis Somoza Debayle took over. He, in turn, remained in power until 1967, when declining health led him to

◀Former Guatemalan dictator Efraín Rios Montt signs an official registration to become a presidential candidate in the election of November 2003. Because Montt was accused of committing genocide during his regime in the early 1980s, which produced thousands of Guatemalan asylum seekers, the country's courts disputed his candidacy.

yield authority to his brother Anastasio Somoza Debayle.

During the late 1940s, the administration of President Harry S. Truman had opposed Anastasio Somoza García's dictatorship. The United States even cut off diplomatic relations with Nicaragua from 1947 to 1948 to protest a puppet regime the dictator had installed.

U.S.-Nicaragua relations warmed somewhat after President Dwight D. Eisenhower took office in 1953, largely because of the Nicaraguan regime's strident anti-communist rhetoric. When Fidel Castro came to power in Cuba in 1959, Luis Somoza Debayle loudly condemned Castro's revolution. He demonstrated that Nicaragua could be relied on as a bulwark against communism, and earned lasting support from the U.S. government, by permitting the Bay of Pigs invasion to be launched from bases on Nicaragua's Caribbean coast.

In the decade and a half that followed the failed invasion, Nicaragua remained a close U.S. ally. By in 1977, a new U.S. president with new foreign policy ideas was inaugurated. President Jimmy Carter sought to make the promotion of human rights a cornerstone of American foreign policy. And Anastasio Somoza Debayle's human rights record was atrocious. Somoza used the National Guard to intimidate, torture, and murder his opponents. Carter criticized these abuses and called for demo-

 Words to Understand in This Chapter

atrocity—an extremely cruel or heinous act.

class action lawsuit—a lawsuit brought on behalf of all members of a large group who share a common interest.

guerrilla—a member of a usually small group of soldiers who do not belong to a regular army and who use tactics such as ambushes, sabotage, raids, and hit-and-run attacks to fight a larger and less mobile traditional military.

Marxist—a communist; specifically, someone who adheres to the theories of Karl Marx, one of the intellectual founders of communism.

Nicaraguan president Anastasio Somoza (1925–80) received U.S. support against the Marxist Sandistinas, but the U.S. government eventually dropped its allegiance, and in 1979 he was deposed and assassinated. Some anti-communist Nicaraguans in the United States were granted asylum, and many were at least protected from deportation.

cratic reforms in Nicaragua. In early 1978, after a prominent Nicaraguan newspaper editor and opposition leader was assassinated—presumably on orders from Somoza—Carter cut off U.S. military aid to Nicaragua.

Since 1972, Somoza's regime had been fighting a revolutionary group, the Frente Sandinista de Liberación Nacional (Sandinista National Liberation Front). The group, commonly known as the Sandinistas, was heavily influenced by Marxist (communist) thinking. The Sandinistas eventually joined with a coalition of democratic, moderate, and non-Marxist groups opposing Somoza.

In June 1979, Sandinista and other opposition leaders formed a provisional government, the Government of National Reconstruction, in neighboring Costa Rica. The following month, when Sandinista rebels finally toppled Somoza's regime, the Government of National Reconstruction declared itself Nicaragua's legitimate government and took power in Managua, the capital.

Nicaragua had been devastated by the years of fighting between Somoza's forces and the rebels. As many as 50,000 Nicaraguans had been killed, and perhaps three times that number had fled the country. The Nicaraguan economy was in shambles.

The new government promised to rebuild the country. It also pledged to bring together Nicaraguans from across the political spectrum. But the Sandinistas soon began marginalizing non-Marxist members of the government and consolidating their power. Within a year, the Sandinistas were firmly in control of the Nicaraguan government. They cultivated close relations with, and accepted aid from, the Soviet Union and Cuba. That drew the ire of the administration of President Ronald Reagan.

In 1981, the year Reagan took office, the United States began funding guerrilla groups seeking to overthrow Nicaragua's Sandinista government. Known as the contras (a shortening of the Spanish word for "counterrevolutionaries"), these groups were largely led by and composed of former members of Nicaragua's National Guard. The contras staged incursions into Nicaragua from bases in neighboring Honduras, where many supporters of Somoza had fled. Although the contras became notorious for atrocities, the Nicaraguan army, too, was implicated in human rights abuses. Both sides often targeted civilians.

The conflict displaced hundreds of thousands of Nicaraguans. From 1981 to 1990, when the fighting ended, about 125,000 Nicaraguans applied for asylum in the United States. Most of them were well educated. During the first half of the 1980s, only about 10 percent of asylum requests by Nicaraguans were granted. But the rate rose dramatically in the latter half of the decade, reaching 27 percent in 1986 and peaking at 84 percent the following year.

El Salvador and Guatemala

Throughout the 1980s, the tiny nation of El Salvador—located to the north of Nicaragua, across the Gulf of Fonseca—was also embroiled in a vicious civil war. The Frente Farabundo Martí para la Liberación Nacional (Farabundo Martí National Liberation Front, FMLN), an umbrella organization made up of five left-wing guerrilla groups, fought to overthrow El Salvador's government. The FMLN was supported by Cuba and Nicaragua. The United States, meanwhile, funneled vast amounts of military and other aid to the Salvadoran government. Ultimately that aid would total about $4 billion.

El Salvador's armed forces pursued a "scorched earth" strategy. In towns and villages where civilians were suspected of helping the FMLN, the army forcibly drove the people from their homes, or sometimes massacred them wholesale. Right-wing

Guatemalan refugees wait for food in a refugee camp in Mexico, 1985. Many people fled the violence in Central American countries like El Salvador, Guatemala, and Nicaragua.

"death squads" kidnapped, tortured, and murdered individuals who spoke out against the government or were believed to hold left-wing sympathies. The FMLN also committed atrocities, though not on the same scale.

To the north of El Salvador, in Guatemala, another civil war raged. It had begun in 1960, six years after a coup organized by the CIA ousted Guatemala's democratically elected but left-wing president. Over the ensuing decades, as a series of military-dominated governments ruled Guatemala, Marxist-inspired guerrillas battled the Guatemalan armed forces, gaining footholds in certain places.

Because of the Guatemalan government's human rights abuses, the administration of President Jimmy Carter had imposed a ban on the sale of U.S. military equipment to Guatemala. But in 1983 the administration of President Ronald Reagan lifted that ban, making the dubious claim that Guatemalan president Efraín

A Nicaraguan rebel turns over his weapon to UN peacekeeping troops as part of a peace agreement in Central America, 1990.

Ríos Montt—a general who'd seized power in a 1982 coup—had taken "significant steps" to improve his country's human rights record. With newly acquired spare parts for their American-made helicopters, Guatemala's armed forces undertook a massive offensive. It targeted not only the guerrillas but also civilians—largely indigenous Mayan peasants—believed to support them. Ríos Montt also drafted some 700,000 Guatemalan men into civilian defense patrols, which made those men and their families targets for retribution from the guerrillas. In just a few years, about 100,000 people were killed, and while the government succeeded in retaking most guerrilla-held territory, the civil war would continue into the mid-1990s.

All told, Guatemala's civil war would claim approximately 200,000 lives. The death toll from El Salvador's civil war, which ended in 1991, is estimated at 75,000.

The brutal conflicts drove millions of people from their

homes. Combined, about a million Salvadorans and Guatemalans entered the United States during the 1980s, most of them illegally.

The Reagan administration (1981–88), which actively supported the governments of Guatemala and El Salvador, portrayed asylum seekers from those countries as economic migrants rather than political refugees. Only 2 to 3 percent of asylum requests from Guatemalans and Salvadorans were granted—far below the rate for Nicaraguan asylum seekers.

In theory, the Refugee Act of 1980 had made it easier for migrants from non-communist countries in Central America to be granted asylum. It seemed apparent, however, that the Reagan administration's foreign policy was coloring asylum decisions—denying Guatemalans and Salvadorans who truly did face persecution in their home countries from receiving protection in the United States.

The Sanctuary Movement and the ABC Case

Some American church groups decided to take the protection of Salvadoran and Guatemalan migrants into their own hands. The groups, collectively known as the Sanctuary movement, began helping the migrants illegally enter the United States. The volunteers described their work as an exercise in civil disobedience, which means they broke laws they considered unjust in order to serve a greater good. Churches hid migrants in church basements, monasteries, and people's homes. They smuggled some people into Canada, where the asylum system was less driven by foreign policy. Sanctuary volunteers, including cofounder Reverend John Fife, were tried and convicted of criminal misconduct. The movement undoubtedly saved lives, and the publicity that accompanied the trials attracted attention to the migrant crisis. Still, government policy concerning the Central Americans did not change.

Other religious groups directly fought the asylum policy in court. In 1985 church and refugee advocacy groups filed a class action lawsuit on behalf of Salvadoran and Guatemalan asylum seekers. Among other things, the lawsuit—known as *American Baptist Churches v. Thornburgh*, or simply the *ABC* Case—alleged that the INS discriminated against Salvadorans and Guatemalans seeking asylum. In 1990 the Department of Justice finally settled the ABC case. Under the terms of the settlement, which was approved by a federal court in January 1991, more than 150,000 Salvadorans and Guatemalans would be eligible to apply for asylum under new rules. The settlement affected people who had already been denied asylum—even those who were served with deportation papers. These people could now reapply for asylum.

In spite of the ABC settlement, some advocates insisted that Guatemalans and Salvadorans still weren't being treated fairly in asylum proceedings, and they pushed for legislation to address the issue. In 1997, after much wrangling in Congress, President Bill Clinton signed the Nicaraguan Adjustment and Central American Relief Act (NACARA). This law made it easier for certain Guatemalan and Salvadoran undocumented migrants—as well as certain Nicaraguans and people of other nationalities—to stay in the United States and eventually apply for permanent resident status.

Text-Dependent Questions

1. What were the Sandinistas?
2. In which Central American country did Efraín Ríos Montt seize power in 1982?
3. What was the Sanctuary movement?

 Research Project

What are conditions like in Nicaragua, Guatemala, and El Salvador today? Research one of those countries and write a two-page report.

5 THE ASYLUM LAW CHANGES OF 1996

J ust days after the inauguration of President Bill Clinton in 1993, a man named Mir Aimal Kansi fired on employees of the CIA outside its headquarters in Langley, Virginia. Bullets hit five people and claimed two lives.

Kansi was a native of Pakistan who had applied for asylum in early 1992. By the time of the shooting, some 11 months later, he had still not gone through an asylum interview to decide his case. The tragedy, in the view of many observers, pointed out the flaws in the asylum system. Asylum officers had been too overwhelmed with other cases to give proper, speedy attention to Kansi's application.

Doubts about the effectiveness of the asylum system were raised again a month later when another asylum applicant was involved in a violent attack. In 1992 Ramzi Yousef, a Pakistani, had been detained at an American airport where he asked for asylum. After making his application, Yousef was allowed to leave. On February 26, 1993, he drove a rented truck filled with explosives into the parking garage of the World Trade Center in New York City. Over 1,000 people were injured by the explosion, and 6 people died.

◀ Emergency workers assist a woman injured in the World Trade Center bombing in February 1993, which killed six people and injured over 1,000 others. Following the bombing, the U.S. asylum system faced criticism after it was revealed that foreign nationals involved in the attack might have been deported, were it not for a massive case backlog that left their asylum claims pending for several months.

Following these incidents, some Americans began to believe that the asylum system was broken. This perception was not entirely unjustified. The system was overloaded. In May 1992, there were 244,000 pending cases; by 1994, the backlog had increased to almost 425,000 cases. People who filed for asylum would sometimes wait years for an interview. While they waited, they were issued temporary papers allowing them to work in the United States until their cases were resolved. The issuence of these papers sometimes allowed those without legitimate claims to exploit the system.

A month after the 1993 World Trade Center bombing, the asylum system's image was dealt yet another blow. William Slattery, a senior INS official in New York, appeared on the television newsmagazine *60 Minutes* to speak about the backlog of cases. The news story drew a correlation between the holes in the asylum system and the recent terrorist attacks, and it portrayed asylum as an easy way to avoid deportation and get working papers. Many human rights advocates believed this broadcast helped shape later criticisms of the U.S. asylum system.

Asylum Reform

One of the advocates for more restrictive asylum laws was Congressman Bill McCollum, a Republican from Florida, who introduced a bill calling for the summary exclusion of asylum seekers. (In the Senate, fellow Republican Alan Simpson of

Words to Understand in This Chapter

expedited removal—the rapid removal from the United States of an alien found to be lacking valid entry documents at a port of entry or along a border.

port of entry—a place where a person may legally enter a country.

voice vote—a vote taken by calling for "ayes" and "noes" and estimating which response is stronger.

Republican Representative Bill McCollum called for tougher asylum laws during the mid-1990s, when he introduced what was known as the "summary exclusion" bill. Portions of his bill, in modified form, became law in 1996.

Wyoming introduced a bill with similar measures.) A proposed solution to the asylum backlog, the summary exclusion provision authorized immigration inspectors at airports and other ports of entry to decide on the spot whether asylum seekers had a legitimate fear of persecution. If asylum seekers were found to have legitimate claims, they would enter the asylum system but usually after a period of detention. If their claims were rejected, they would be sent back to their home country on the next plane. (*A Well-Founded Fear: The Congressional Battle to Save Political Asylum in America*, written by Georgetown University Law School professor Philip Schrag, is the best book on the changes to political asylum in the 1990s and the source of much of the information provided here.)

Summary exclusion had been brought before Congress and the Senate before. During the Reagan administration, when the asylum backlog had just begun to grow, Senator Simpson had proposed similar changes to the asylum system as part of a broader immigration bill. Simpson also had proposed a 30-day deadline to apply for asylum. He asserted that someone coming to the United States for protection should know the reason and be able to declare it within a month.

Refugee advocacy organizations and attorneys who represented asylum seekers claimed that Simpson's proposals were unfair and ill advised, and the proposals were ultimately rejected by the Democrat-controlled Senate. When the Immigration Reform and Control Act was passed in 1986, it did not include any changes to asylum law.

By 1995, however, political conditions were different. Overall, the public was more skeptical of asylum seekers' motivations. And crucially, Republicans now controlled Congress. Simpson judged that the time was right to reintroduce his proposed changes to U.S. asylum law.

Cutting Down the Case Backlog

The Clinton administration hired immigration expert David Martin as a consultant to reform the asylum system. Martin was a law professor and under the Carter administration had worked on Haitian asylum cases for the State Department's human rights office. In 1995 Martin developed a number of procedural reforms to eliminate the backlog and to allow the asylum system to run more smoothly.

The new regulations gave asylum officers 180 days to complete a case before work papers were issued. This doubled the amount of time the system had to process claims. In addition, asylum applicants were not given automatic work authorization while their application was pending, thus removing the incentive to file asylum solely to gain legal work status. Finally, the most recently filed applications would be handled first, and the backlog would be dealt with as time permitted. This made it much less likely that an applicant would get work authorization simply because officers failed to meet the deadline.

The new changes made a big difference. After they took effect in January 1995, new asylum applications dropped 44 percent. Ironically, once much of the fraud

Republican Senator Alan Simpson fought for immigration restrictions in the 1980s and 1990s. In 1996, asylum restrictions proposed by Simpson and others were written into law with the passing of the Illegal Immigration Reform and Immigrant Responsibility Act (IIRIRA).

had been removed from the system, the asylum approval rate increased.

A New Republican Majority

Despite the success of the reforms, from a political standpoint they had arrived too late. The 1994 congressional elections gave the Republican Party control of the Senate and the House of Representatives. The Republican majorities would craft and pass the historic 1996 Illegal Immigration Reform and Immigrant Responsibility Act (IIRIRA).

On January 24, 1995, Alan Simpson introduced an immigration bill in the Senate. It dealt with a number of issues covering both legal and undocumented immigrants. The bill included a cap on the number of refugees allowed into the United States each year, as well as provisions for summary exclusion. It also brought another old proposal of Simpson's back to the table—a deadline for asylum seekers. Philip Schrag notes how these measures were problematic for legitimate asylum seekers. The most restrictive measure was the 30-day deadline for asylum applications, which threatened to prevent many deserving applicants from receiving asylum.

Most asylum seekers require more than 30 days to apply for asylum. There are a few reasons for this. One, asylum seekers may not yet know what asylum is, or how to get it; some may expect that they receive it automatically upon reaching U.S. shores. Two, the asylum system is intimidating, especially to the people who need it the most. To get help filling out the application form, many asylees seek a lawyer or representative, which takes time, especially if they don't speak English. Thirty days can seem like a long time, but in a foreign country with an unfamiliar language and set of customs, it's often not a long enough period to find the right legal assistance.

The House Bill

Representative Lamar Smith, a Texas Republican who chaired the House Immigration Subcommittee, coordinated with Senator

Simpson on the asylum reforms. Smith introduced a bill similar to Simpson's in the House. After a bill like this is introduced, it goes into the markup process in the relevant committee. During markup, committee members debate changes to the bill that are voted on by the entire committee.

Lobbyists also try to convince legislators to vote a certain way during this stage. The House and Senate immigration bills sparked the creation of a new lobby group—the Committee to Protect Asylum (CPA), made up primarily of human rights and legal organizations. A founding member of the committee, Philip Schrag documents its goals and methods in *A Well-Founded Fear*. Members of the CPA wrote letters to newspapers, called congressional offices, and brought asylees to face-to-face meetings with legislators. Their main goal was to eliminate the asylum deadline and modify other provisions.

The Senate Bill

During the markup stage of the asylum bill debate, the Senate bill had been modified more than the House bill. The asylum deadline in the Senate bill was extended from 30 days to one year. Also, it applied only to people making defensive asylum claims against being deported, and exceptions to the deadline could be made if asylum seekers showed "good cause." These exceptions included physical or mental disabilities, fear for one's family abroad, changed circumstances in the applicant's country of origin, or the unavailability of professional assistance. The INS was also allowed to add more exceptions as it saw fit.

In addition, the Senate bill repealed the summary exclusion procedures that had been included in a recently passed anti-terrorism bill. Earlier in the year, the House had drafted and passed an anti-terrorism bill that included broad summary exclusion powers. Although it was presented as a terrorism bill, the summary exclusion provision had not been limited to terrorists and people suspected of terrorism, but applied to anyone who entered the United States without the proper documents. The immigration bill that reached the House floor was more restrictive, letting the summary exclusion provisions stand. Also, the asylum deadline was set at six months, and it applied to people making both affirmative and defensive claims.

Finding a Compromise

The next stage in the legislative process was to reconcile the House and Senate bills. This is done in a conference committee, which includes members of both chambers of Congress. Often members of both parties work out a compromise, ironing out the differences between the two bills. In the case of the immigration bill, something different happened. In his account of the events, Schrag contends that the Republicans from the House and the Senate met in private, making agreements in a series of pre-conference meetings. When the full conference committee met at last, most differences had been worked out with no input from the Democratic legislators.

The conference itself was largely a formality. The bill had already been written, and the conference committee's chairman, Lamar Smith, allowed no Democratic amendments to be heard. The bill that emerged was severe in a number of areas, using the more restrictive House bill as the main text. Some other changes were made. The term "summary exclusion" changed to "expedited removal," though with only one major difference, the provision basically retained the same function. Expedited removal would apply to anyone stopped at a port of entry without a visa or passport, but not to others. The one difference was that people who contested their expedited removal would have the right to appeal, although they were allowed a week to prepare their case. The asylum deadline was extended to one full year, but the Senate's detailed definition of having "good cause" to file late was struck from the bill.

A New Law

On September 28, 1996, the House of Representatives passed the Illegal Immigration Reform and Immigrant Responsibility Act (IIRIRA) with a vote of 370 to 37. Two days later, the Senate

passed IIRIRA on a voice vote, and President Clinton signed the bill into law.

When the president signs a bill, it often seems like the end of the story. In reality, this is just the beginning in many ways. After the law is signed, it must be put into practice. There are many steps between the broad language of a law and the act of enforcing it. In other words, once a law is written everyone must comply; however, many laws leave some room for interpretation.

Philip Schrag describes how at the enforcement level, asylum advocates tempered some of the harsher provisions of the 1996 act. The INS was convinced to apply broader interpretations to the two exceptions to the one-year deadline, which fell under the designations "changed circumstances" and "extraordinary circumstances." The regulations set out specific conditions under which these exceptions would apply and gave asylum officers discretion within the framework of the regulations.

Also, the regulations stated that expedited removal would only be used on people who were stopped at ports of entry without the right documents. It would not be used for people who did not use ports of entry—such as the many Mexican border crossings (though expedited removal would later be expanded to include these people)—or for those who were approved to enter the country but were later deemed deportable.

The immigration laws of the 1990s introduced stringent measures, but those measures were eased somewhat in their execution. In effect, the long battle over political asylum had ended in a draw.

 Text-Dependent Questions

1. Why did the asylum requests of Mir Aimal Kamsi and Ramzi Ahmed Yousef help change American public opinion regarding the asylum system?

2. What changes to U.S. asylum procedures were championed by Senator Alan Simpson?

3. Name the 1996 law that reformed asylum in the United States.

 Research Project

Find out what happened to Ramzi Yousef. Where and how was he caught? Where is he today?

THE ASYLUM PROCESS, STEP BY STEP

The Illegal Immigration Reform and Immigrant Responsibility Act was an important law with significant consequences for asylum seekers. It wasn't, however, the last word from Congress on asylum.

In 2005, Congress passed an emergency spending bill to which it attached a measure known as the REAL ID Act. On May 11, 2005, President George W. Bush signed the bill into law.

The primary goal of the REAL ID Act was to decrease the country's vulnerability to terrorism. The law sought to make it impossible for foreign terrorists to use phony American driver's licenses or other state-issued forms of identification, with which they could board airplanes or otherwise travel easily around the country.

But the REAL ID Act also imposed a higher burden of proof on asylum seekers. It requires asylum seekers to demonstrate clearly "that race, religion, nationality, membership in a particular social group, or political opinion was or will be at least one central reason for persecuting the applicant." In addition, even when an asylum seeker's testimony is credible, the law allows the adjudicator (whether an asylum officer or immigration judge) to require corroborating evidence, unless the asylum

◄ A U.S. Navy ship transports Cuban refugees who were picked up at sea while trying to reach the United States. In recent decades, hundreds of thousands of migrants from Caribbean countries like Cuba, the Dominican Republic, and Haiti have attempted to reach the United States in ships, boats, and even rafts.

seeker can't reasonably obtain that evidence. Under the REAL ID Act, adjudicators are also given much more latitude to determine that an asylum seeker isn't credible. For example, minor inaccuracies or inconsistencies in the person's story can weigh against the asylum seeker—even when those inaccuracies or inconsistencies aren't relevant to the actual asylum claim.

Unlike refugees, asylum applicants get to the United States on their own power. They only apply for asylum once they have arrived. U.S. law allows any number of people to be granted asylum in a year; however, under the law, a maximum of 10,000 asylees may become lawful permanent residents in a given year.

Asylees arrive in a number of ways. Some arrive illegally, desperate to escape the dangerous conditions of their homeland. Others arrive legally on temporary visas, and decide to apply for asylum only after learning their country has recently become a dangerous place to live.

Some immigrant groups, like those from Cuba, the Dominican Republic, and Haiti, are close enough to sail to the United States. They may use their own boats or travel with a neighbor or family, or they may contact professional smugglers, who charge a high price for transport.

Some people stow away on airplanes. Flying in this manner is particularly dangerous, with the cold temperatures at high altitudes dropping to 60 degrees below zero. In 1997, two Indian men stowed away in an airplane's wheel compartment. One man survived the 10-hour flight, but his younger brother froze to death and fell from the plane. In December 2002, a man also successfully flew from Cuba to Canada in a wheel well. The

 Words to Understand in This Chapter

adjudicator—a person with the power to judge or decide a contested issue. corroborating—providing confirmation or support.

impunity—freedom from punishment or consequences.

week before, two boys from the African country of Ghana tried the same method of escape, but both died from the lack of oxygen and freezing temperatures.

Leaving a hostile country can be as challenging a problem as arriving in a safe one. Families often offer aid in the escape. People will bribe guards to set imprisoned family members free. Additional money and connections will go a long way toward finally getting someone out of the country. Assistance can come from strangers as well as friends and family—supporters of the Sanctuary movement of the 1980s volunteered to smuggle Guatemalans and Salvadorans into the United States, for example. It is also common for sympathetic groups to provide false passports and money for a plane ticket.

Arrival

Asylum seekers may discover that their ordeal has not ended upon arriving in North America. U.S. asylum procedures are complicated and full of obstacles to a successful claim. As one scholar noted recently, "Enduring the asylum process is not easy."

Under the expedited removal provisions of the Illegal Immigration Reform and Immigrant Responsibility Act, noncitizens who enter the United States without the proper documents (such as a valid passport or visa) may be subject to quick deportation without a hearing before an immigration judge. Expedited removal is most often used at ports of entry (international airports, sea ports, and official land crossings). However, migrants who arrive in the United States by sea but not at a port of entry, or who are interdicted at sea, may also be placed in expedited removal proceedings. So, too, may any undocumented immigrant who is apprehended within 100 miles of the U.S. border with Mexico or Canada.

Some undocumented immigrants request asylum immediately upon encountering U.S. authorities. If they don't, however, Customs and Border Patrol agents are required to ask why they've come to the United States and whether they're afraid to return to their home country. Those who express a fear of returning to their home country cannot be deported immediately. However, complaints filed in 2013 by the American Immigration Lawyers' Association and in 2014 by the National Immigrant Justice Center and nine other civil rights and immigration legal-aid groups, alleged systemic problems at the southern border. According to the complaints, agents sometimes failed to ask undocumented immigrants whether they feared returning to their home countries, or refused to record positive responses to that question, or improperly informed migrants that they didn't have a legitimate asylum claim. In other cases, the complaints alleged, agents inaccurately reported what they were told, ensuring discrepancies with the migrants' later statements and often dooming their asylum applications.

When an undocumented immigrant does express a fear of returning to his or her home country (and that fear is recorded), the person is immediately placed in detention pending a "credible fear" interview. In order to give the migrant time to prepare, the interview takes place no sooner than 48 hours later (unless the migrant waives the waiting period). Depending on circumstances, it may take weeks before the credible fear interview occurs.

Credible Fear Interview

The responsibility for conducting credible fear interviews falls to asylum officers, who are employees of U.S. Citizenship and Immigration Services. When the foreign national isn't a native English-speaker, which is usually the case, an interpreter is present to translate questions and answers.

The asylum officer begins the interview by asking general questions, such as the person's date of birth and the place where he or she formerly lived. Then the interview turns to why the person fears returning to his or her country. The asylum officer will ask specifically whether the person has ever been threatened or harmed because of his or her race or ethnicity, religion, nationality, membership in a specific social group, or political

Asian migrants are discovered by U.S. Coast Guardsmen in the cargo hold of a ship in the northern Hawaiian Islands, 1999. Stowing away in a ship or plane is a typical—though often dangerous—method of illegal migration.

opinion. Has the person ever faced torture or severe mistreatment at the hands of the government?

There might be little doubt that the person has fled terrible violence. The person may truly expect to be harmed or even killed if returned to his or her country. But that isn't necessarily relevant. The motivation behind the violence or the threat must fall into one of the categories that would mark the person as a refugee. If not, the asylum officer may decide the person has no legal claim to protection in the United States. This harsh reality was illustrated by a crisis that exploded in 2014.

Beginning in 2009, a steadily increasing number of undocumented migrants from Mexico and three Central American countries—El Salvador, Guatemala, and Honduras—had started requesting asylum in the United States. Then, between 2013 and 2014, the numbers nearly doubled.

Most of the migrants said they were fleeing violence perpetrated by criminal gangs, many of which were involved in the illegal-drug trade. These gangs routinely kidnapped, raped, and murdered girls and women. Often, they killed young males who refused to join their ranks. They targeted the families of anyone who tried to bring them to justice, including police, and in many areas the gangs operated with virtual impunity. Gangs were a primary driver of shockingly high levels of violence in Central America. According to a UN report, Honduras had by far the highest murder rate in the world in 2012. El Salvador, meanwhile, had the world's fourth highest murder rate, and Guatemala the fifth highest. Overall, Mexico's homicide rate wasn't as high. But certain states where the country's powerful drug cartels operated did suffer from extreme violence.

Despite these grim facts, the overwhelming majority of Honduran, Guatemalan, Salvadoran, and Mexican asylum claims were denied (according to a 2010 study by Syracuse University's Transactional Records Access Clearinghouse, the denial rate ranged from nearly 86 percent for Mexicans to more than 90 percent for Salvadorans). In the view of immigration officials, most Central American and Mexican asylum seekers were trying to escape crime in general rather than persecution directed specifically at them. "We'll have a very difficult time being able to say no to any person who claims to flee a country because of criminal conditions," a former immigration judge noted.

In addition to probing the reasons a migrant says he or she is afraid to return home, an asylum officer conducting a credible fear interview will try to ascertain whether certain factors automatically disqualify the person from being granted asylum. For example, U.S. law prohibits asylum for anyone who has persecuted others in his or her home country; has been convicted of a serious crime, or is strongly suspected of committing one, outside the United States; or has ever engaged in, incited, or supported terrorism.

At the end of a credible fear interview, the asylum officer will usually ask the migrant whether he or she has anything to add. After the migrant has spoken, the interview concludes.

The asylum officer then sets about rendering a written decision. If the officer concludes that the migrant has a credible fear of being persecuted or tortured, that doesn't mean the person is granted asylum. It simply means that he or she can apply for asylum. Credible fear interviews are screening procedures; asylum cases are ultimately decided in immigration court.

However, a negative credible fear decision doesn't necessarily end a migrant's chances of obtaining asylum. The person may request that an immigration judge review the decision. If the judge agrees with the asylum officer, there is no appeal. The person is promptly deported by Immigration and Customs Enforcement (ICE).

Parole and Detention

After receiving an affirmative credible fear decision, an asylum seeker may ask to be paroled (released from detention). But parole is by no means automatic. Decisions are made by local ICE officials, and studies have found huge differences in parole rates around the country. In some places, fewer than 5 percent of applicants have been granted parole; in other places, nearly everyone has been paroled. And there's another reason refugee advocates say parole is inherently unfair: in general, only undocumented immigrants who've presented an asylum claim at a port of entry or have been apprehended near a border are subject to detention in the first place. Undocumented immigrants who make an asylum claim after being in the country are detained only under rare circumstances.

For a detained asylum seeker, not receiving parole can mean spending months or even years in a jail-like, often overcrowded detention center while awaiting an immigration hearing. That, obviously, leads to significant misery. But it can also negatively affect the asylum seeker's chances of getting asylum. According to refugee advocates, many detainees give up otherwise-promising asylum claims and accept deportation after becoming disheartened by a long period of confinement. In addition, detention tends to make it harder for an asylum seeker to get a lawyer (particularly since many detention centers are located in remote areas). Studies have shown that less than one in six detainees is represented by legal counsel—yet immigration judges are almost three times more likely to grant asylum to applicants with lawyers.

Immigration Court

People who have filed an affirmative asylum application (after being in the United States for some time) are scheduled to appear at one of USCIS's Asylum Offices. There are eight such offices (located in Arlington, Virginia; Chicago; Houston; Los Angeles; Miami; Newark, New Jersey; New York City; and San Francisco). At the office, an asylum officer interviews the asylum seeker at length and reviews the facts of the case. Later (generally after a few weeks), the asylum seeker is called to return to the Asylum Office, where he or she is given a letter noting whether or not the asylum claim has been approved. If it hasn't, the asylum seeker's case is automatically referred to immigration court for removal proceedings.

Like typical court cases in the United States, those proceedings—whether involving a person whose affirmative asylum claim has been denied or a person who was apprehended by the authorities and placed in expedited removal—are adversarial. A lawyer representing the government (usually from ICE) argues the case for the asylum seeker's removal from the country. A lawyer representing the asylum seeker—or the asylum seeker representing himself or herself—argues the case for the granting of asylum. Evidence is introduced, and witnesses testify and are cross-examined. An immigration judge presides over the hearing, which may last a few hours or stretch over several days.

At the end of the proceedings, the immigration judge verbally announces his or her decision. If asylum is denied, the person does have an avenue of appeal, but success is not likely. If asylum is granted, however, a new chapter in the immigrant's story begins.

 # Text-Dependent Questions

1. What is the annual limit on the number of asylees granted permanent resident status in the United States?
2. How did the REAL ID Act of 2005 affect asylum seekers?
3. Where are affirmative asylum seekers first interviewed?

 # Research Project

Find recent figures for the number of asylum seekers from Central America and Mexico. Present the information in graph form.

7 Life in the New World

For those who have grown up in a different culture, adjusting to life in the United States can be a challenge. People speak a different language. A lot of food comes in plastic packages, and much of it is unhealthy. All consumers are faced with thousands of choices, and there are risky temptations, such as the immediate buying power offered by credit cards.

While asylees are adjusting to life in the United States, they are also coping with shattered lives. Loved ones are either dead or worlds removed from the United States. During the months—in some cases, years—before finding protection, asylees saw and did things they might have managed to briefly forget. But once they finally reach relative safety, those thoughts and fears tend to return. People may suffer from recurring nightmares, or become clinically depressed.

Asylees typically go through similar psychological states, regardless of where they have come from. Initially, they may go through a brief period of euphoria. Life in the United States is strange and new, but it feels safe, and the process of settling in requires too much attention to stop and dwell on the horrors of the past.

Soon, however, this new life proves to be not as easy as it

◀ Cuban newcomers share stories at the counter of a restaurant in Miami, Florida. Asylees often look to their own ethnic community for support during the difficult period of adjustment in their new country.

first seemed. Many asylees fall into a deep depression. Their loss sinks in—perhaps they have lost friends, husbands, wives, or children, and they may never see their homeland again. As they finally start to cope with their loss, pressures from their new life close in. They might have figured out the basics of their new country, but there is still a lot they don't understand.

Making it through this period is difficult. But after spending a few years in the United States, most people have begun rebuilding their lives. They have made friends, and put down some tentative roots in their new country. The feelings of loss remain, yet many asylees have found a way to cope.

Potential Problems

Certain aspects of living in the United States may place strains on asylee families. Different forces can draw the family apart. Parents typically work long hours for low pay, which will put food on the table but may put distance between children and parents.

Many asylee men and women often have trouble adjusting to gender role differences in American society. Women may have more responsibilities and freedoms in the home and the workplace than men are accustomed to. Power also can shift between the old and young. When children pick up English faster than their parents, they can slowly become the "family translator." During early stages of resettlement, the children's grasp of English can be very useful, but it can ultimately threaten the family structure. In having control over the information, the

 Words to Understand in This Chapter

euphoria—a feeling of intense excitement and happiness.

proficiency—advanced skill at a task or in a particular area.

war crimes—acts that violate international laws governing the conduct of warfare.

children can acquire more power than is customary. If the parents fall behind their children in English proficiency, conflicts can arise between generations.

Success and Service

Despite the obstacles asylees face, it is impossible to discount their spirit. The same fortitude they used to pull themselves out of their country can be used in making a new life. Some eventually pull the resources together to open their own businesses.

The diverse U.S. economy has provided opportunities for many asylees. Some are able to buy homes within a few years of arrival. They lmay take advantage of government loans available to low-income buyers. Many asylees with regular jobs are able to make regular payments on loans and build good credit ratings. Although they may only have had one or two years of a legitimate financial history, this is often enough for some banks to hand out loans. Some asylees receive loans even before they received permanent resident status.

A number of asylees have become politically active, working for human rights causes, or documenting war crimes in their homeland. Performing this kind of work has been rewarding for many refugees and asylees and has helped them maintain their connection to their homeland.

 Text-Dependent Questions

1. Why do some asylees become depressed after being in the United States for a while?
2. What are some potential strains on the family life of asylees?
3. What are some ways asylees have translated their experience into political activity?

 Research Project

Using the Internet, find the story of an asylum seeker. List all the obstacles the person had to overcome to gain asylum.

8 Asylum in the Spotlight

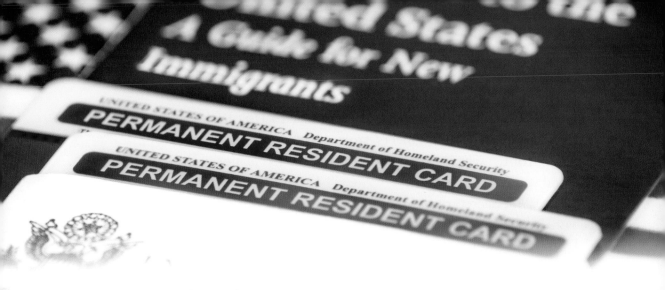

The identities of people who receive asylum are generally kept private, in accordance with U.S. law. Only when an asylee waives his or her right to privacy do others know that he or she has received asylum. Nonetheless, there have been some famous asylum cases.

Since childhood, Wernher von Braun, a German born in 1912, had been fascinated by the idea of spaceflight. Specifically, von Braun dreamed of landing people on the moon. During the early 1930s, von Braun graduated from a technical institute in Berlin and went on to obtain a PhD in physics. His experiments with rockets drew the attention of Germany's Nazi regime, and during World War II von Braun was put in charge of a team of German scientists and engineers tasked with developing rockets for use as offensive weapons. They created a powerful rocket, called the V-2, which was capable of flying 500 miles and delivering a one-ton warhead.

At a social gathering in 1944, von Braun predicted that Germany would lose the war and confessed that he'd only ever wanted to build rockets to launch them into space. Those comments were reported to the Gestapo, Nazi Germany's secret police, which viewed them as tantamount to treason. Von Braun was arrested.

◀ Cuban Americans demonstrate outside the home of Elián González' relatives in Miami, April 2000. Thousands of Cuban Americans in Miami and other communities supported Elián's relatives in their fight to let the boy remain in the United States.

Von Braun's partner, Walter Dornberger, convinced the Gestapo that it should not keep von Braun interned, and he was released. Soon afterward, von Braun gathered his staff and held a meeting. They collectively agreed to surrender to U.S. forces. Using forged papers, the engineers stole a train to reach the American front, where they encountered an American private and surrendered to him.

In June 1945, Secretary of State Edward R. Stettinius agreed to let von Braun and his remaining engineers immigrate to the United States. However, their migration would be kept confidential. As part of Operation Paperclip, each approved transfer was secretly marked with a paperclip atop the file. Von Braun and 126 other German scientists were eventually transferred to the United States.

Whether or not von Braun and the others would qualify as asylees under today's laws and procedures is hard to say, but their skills did prove valuable to the United States. They instructed U.S. soldiers on how to detect and avoid a rocket attack.

Von Braun, who was granted citizenship in 1955, continued his rocketry research in the United States. His teams built the Jupiter-C and Pershing missiles for the army, and on January 31, 1958, von Braun's team launched the first U.S. satellite, *Explorer 1*. Von Braun later directed the Saturn rocket program, which helped launch American astronauts to the moon in 1969.

Operation Paperclip proved to the U.S. government that there was a strategic benefit to providing asylum for people like von Braun and his colleagues. During the Cold War, the political

 Words to Understand in This Chapter

defect—to renounce one's country and go to another, usually for ideological reasons.

elite—the most successful or powerful people in a society.

totalitarian—relating to a repressive system in which the government seeks to control all aspects of people's lives.

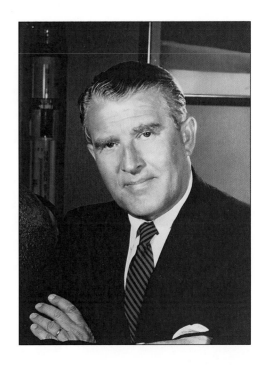

Dr. Wernher von Braun (1912–77), a German rocket scientist, gave himself up to U.S. forces during World War II. He received asylum, and shortly after becoming a U.S. citizen, led the project to launch the first U.S. satellite, *Explorer 1*, in January 1958.

act of granting asylum retained its strategic value. Many Western countries provided asylum for famous artists, entertainers, and athletes from communist countries. Celebrities helped put a face on asylum for the general public. Their defections also supported the view that the Soviet government was oppressive and totalitarian. After all, if the cultural elite were persecuted, how much worse was it for the average person?

The Soviet Union

Russian dancer Rudolf Nureyev was one of those persecuted elite. As a Leningrad ballet student in the 1950s, he refused to attend meetings of the communist youth group called the Komsomol. But Nureyev shined on the ballet stage, earning a role as a soloist for the Leningrad Kiro Ballet soon after he graduated in 1958. Three years later, he slipped away from his touring company (and its Soviet guards) in France, and requested asylum at an airport. After receiving asylum, Nureyev took the opportunity to travel around the world, dancing in *Swan Lake*, *The Nutcracker*, and *Lucifer*, for which he had the title role.

Ballet dancer Mikhail Baryshnikov (right) defected from the former Soviet Union and was granted asylum.

Two decades later, another Soviet dancer followed in Nureyev's footsteps. Mikhail Baryshnikov defected in 1974, during a dance tour in Toronto. He claimed that the Soviet Union's repressive system denied artists the freedom of expression, and that he was not allowed to perform many contemporary pieces. The Canadian government decided to grant him asylum.

In the West, Baryshnikov became a member of the American Ballet Theatre, choreographing and dancing in *The Nutcracker* and *Don Quixote*. In addition to becoming one of the most recognized contemporary dancers, he starred in movies such as *That's Dancing!* and *White Nights*, in which he played a Russian dancer who receives asylum in the United States.

Another Soviet defector was grandmaster chess player Viktor Korchnoi. During a 1976 chess tournament in Amsterdam, Korchnoi defected and was granted asylum in the Netherlands.

A Brave Escape

Each of these cases was, in some way, a public relations victory against communism. In contrast, the asylum granted to Fauziya Kassindja in 1996 was a victory for compassion.

Fauziya was a teenager when she fled Africa with the help of her sister and mother. She was the youngest daughter of a wealthy Muslim family in Togo. Her father was a progressive thinker, and sent his daughters to boarding school for a better education. He would not consider letting his daughters marry unless they truly loved their suitors. What's more, he would not let his daughters undergo the traditional *kakia* procedure. Sometimes called "female circumcision," *kakia* is a brutal ritual. It is a painful and sometimes fatal mutilation of a female's—usually a 15-year-old girl's—genital area.

While Fauziya was at boarding school, her father died. The power in the family passed to Fauziya's uncle. He and his wife drove Fauziya's mother away and then claimed custody of Fauziya and her younger brother. More traditional in their child-raising approach, the aunt and uncle took Fauziya out of boarding school and made plans for her to marry a 45-year-old man who already had three wives. Fauziya resisted, but one day she was told marriage preparations would begin, and in two days, she would undergo the *kakia*.

Fauziya was terrified, but felt powerless to stop it. The night before the *kakia* ceremony, her older sister helped her escape. Giving her money their mother had saved, Fauziya's sister led her into Ghana, where she arranged for a smuggler to get Fauziya on a flight to Germany. Once she was past German customs, she was on her own.

A kindhearted woman took Fauziya in, and eventually she made another friend who suggested that she apply for asylum. Since Fauziya spoke English but no German, the friend arranged for her to apply in the United States. Fauziya touched down at a U.S. airport on December 17, 1994. She asked for asylum almost immediately. However, when she told her story to the officer interviewing her, she left out details of the *kakia*. Fauziya was modest, and the story was too personal to relate.

Consequently, the initial report said that Fauziya left her country because she didn't want to marry the man her aunt had picked out, which was hardly worthy of asylum. Instead of receiving asylum, she endured 16 months in an INS detention center. Eventually, she made contact with law student Layli Miller Bashir and attorney Karen Musalo. They agreed to represent Fauziya in immigration court, where they fought a long legal battle to get her asylum.

The key was getting *kakia* recognized as a form of persecution. One important step was replacing the euphemism "female circumcision," which sounded medical and thus gave it false credibility. Bashir and Musalo worked to replace the term with the more explicit "female genital mutilation." FGM was eventually recognized as a form of persecution, grounds under which Fauziya could receive asylum. With this court victory, one immigrant had helped change the asylum system.

The Debate over Elián

Another groundbreaking asylum case was that of Elián González. In November 1999, six-year-old Elián was rescued at sea off the coast of Florida. His mother had brought him with her as she fled Cuba. Their boat capsized and Elián's mother drowned, but he survived and was picked up by a fisherman. Soon Elián was paroled into the country. His great-uncle, who lived in Miami, claimed custody of him and filed an asylum application on Elián's behalf.

Meanwhile Elián's father, who was divorced from his mother, learned what had happened and requested that his son be returned to Cuba. The asylum application was now open to debate. Who should speak on behalf of Elián—his great-uncle in the United States, or his father in Cuba? Elián said he wanted to stay in the United States, but it hadn't been established yet if a child could apply for asylum against his parents' wishes. The legal battle over Elián moved from court to court.

Protesters hold signs near the family home of Elián Gonzalez on April 14, 2000 in Little Havana, Florida.

On the morning of April 23, Justice Department agents stormed the home of Elián's uncle. Armed agents took Elián from his relatives and returned him to his father. In June, the U.S. Supreme Court refused to overturn a circuit court ruling against the relatives, ending the case. Elián and his father returned home to Cuba.

The World-Trotting Cyclist

Another asylum case that garnered news attention is that of Reza Baluchi, an Iranian national who has devoted himself to bicycling around the world to promote peace. He had been a member of Iran's bicycling team and served his required term in the military. Baluchi began to attend some unrecognized political meetings in his country, for which he was arrested and tortured. After several more arrests, one of which led to a one-and-a-half

year stint in prison ending in 1996, Baluchi decided to leave the country.

Reza Baluchi is an Iranian athlete and activist who received asylum in the United States.

He left on his bicycle, and for seven years pedaled almost all over the world. On November 10, 2002, Baluchi was picked up by U.S. Border Patrol agents. He had mistakenly ridden his bike across the U.S.-Mexico border while waiting for his U.S. visa to be approved. He had plans to ride to the World Trade Center memorial site in New York City, arriving on September 11, 2003, the second anniversary of the terrorist attacks.

Baluchi was detained for five months while his case was decided. He ran in the prison yard to keep in shape for his upcoming ride. While he was detained he promised that after he was released he would finish the peace tour on foot, running from Los Angeles to New York. In February 2003, Baluchi's asylum was approved, and as promised, he left Los Angeles in May, ran 30 to 40 miles a day, and arrived in New York on September 11.

Cuban Baseball Players

Of course, not every asylum applicant is accepted, and not every celebrity defector becomes an asylee. In the summer of 2000, two Cuban baseball players—Andy Morales and Carlos Borrego—were discovered with 29 others aboard a smuggling ship headed to the United States. The ship had run out of gas, and its passengers tried to buy fuel from a passing boat. Instead of giving them fuel, the boat's captain radioed the Coast Guard.

Neither Morales nor Borrego established the "credible fear" that would have merited asylum. All of the boat's passengers were turned back to Cuba. Other Cuban baseball players have been granted asylum in the United States, but Morales was the first high-profile Cuban star to be rejected.

There are sure to be more famous asylum cases in the future. But for every asylum case that makes the news, there are thousands more that do not, and there is as much at stake in an anonymous case as there is in the most public: liberty, the pursuit of happiness, and, quite possibly, someone's life.

 Text-Dependent Questions

1. Name the famous ballet dancer who was granted asylum in Canada in 1974.
2. From what country did Fauziya Kassindja escape? What was she fleeing?
3. How did Elián González arrive in the United States? What ultimately happened to him?

 Research Project

Choose a famous asylee (either someone discussed in this chapter or another person who interests you). Write a brief biography.

Series Glossary of Key Terms

assimilate—to adopt the ways of another culture; to fully become part of a different country or society.

census—an official count of a country's population.

deport—to forcibly remove someone from a country, usually back to his or her native land.

green card—a document that denotes lawful permanent resident status in the United States.

migrant laborer—an agricultural worker who travels from region to region, taking on short-term jobs.

naturalization—the act of granting a foreign-born person citizenship.

passport—a paper or book that identifies the holder as the citizen of a country; usually required for traveling to or through other foreign lands.

undocumented immigrant—a person who enters a country without official authorization; sometimes referred to as an "illegal immigrant."

visa—official authorization that permits arrival at a port of entry but does not guarantee admission into the United States.

Further Reading

Bahrampour, Tara. *To See and See Again: A Life in Iran and America*. New York: Farrar, Strauss, and Giroux, 1999.

Bourke, Dale Hanson. *Immigration: Tough Questions, Direct Answers*. Downers Grove, IL: InterVarsity Press, 2014.

Castles, Stephen, and Mark J. Miller. *The Age of Migration*, 2nd ed. New York: The Guilford Press, 1998.

Chomsky, Aviva. *Undocumented: How Immigration Became Illegal*. Boston: Beacon Press, 2014.

Einolf, Christopher J. *The Mercy Factory: Refugees and the American Asylum System*. Chicago, Ill.: Ivan R. Dee, 2001.

Gjelten, Tom. *A Nation of Nations: A Great American Immigration Story*. New York: Simon and Schuster, 2015.

Gonzalez-Pando, Miguel. *The Cuban Americans*. Westport, Conn.: Greenwood Press, 1998.

Kassindja, Fauziya, and Layli Miller Bashir. *Do They Hear You When You Cry*. New York: Delacorte Press, 1998.

Kenney, David Ngaruri, and Philip G. Schrag. *Asylum Denied: A Refugee's Struggle for Safety in America*. Berkeley and Los Angeles: University of California Press, 2008.

Laguerre, Michel S. *Haitian Americans in Transnational America*. New York: St. Martin's Press, 1998.

Little, Allan, and Laura Silber. *Yugoslavia: Death of a Nation*. New York: Penguin Books, 1997.

Loescher, Gil, and John A. Scanlan. *Calculated Kindness*. New York: The Free Press, 1986.

McClellan, Grant S., ed. *Immigrants, Refugees, and U.S. Policy*. New York: H. W. Wilson Company, 1981.

Merino, Noel. *Illegal Immigration*. San Diego: Greenhaven Press, 2015.

Miller, Banks; Linda Camp Keith; and Jennifer S. Holmes. *Immigration Judges and U.S. Asylum Policy*. Philadelphia: University of Pennsylvania Press, 2014.

Pipher, Mary. *The Middle of Everywhere: The World's Refugees Come to Our Town*. New York: Harcourt, 2002.

Schrag, Philip G. *A Well-Founded Fear: The Congressional Battle to Save Political Asylum in America*. New York: Routledge, 2000.

Shawcross, William. *The Quality of Mercy*. New York: Simon and Schuster, 1984.

Suleiman, Michael W., ed. *Arabs in America: Building a New Future*. Philadelphia: Temple University Press, 1999.

United Nations High Commissioner for Refugees. *The State of the World's Refugees*. Oxford: Oxford University Press, 2012.

Zucker, Norman L., and Naomi Flink Zucker. *Desperate Crossings: Seeking Refuge in America*. Armonk, N.Y.: M.E. Sharpe, 1996.

Internet Resources

www.uscis.gov/humanitarian/refugees-asylum/asylum

Detailed information on asylum in the United States, from U.S. Citizenship and Immigration Services.

www.canadianhistory.ca/iv/main.html

This site contains an excellent history of immigration to Canada from the 1800s to the present.

www.hrw.org/topic/refugees

The home site of Human Rights Watch is an up-to-date resource covering refugee issues and the recent campaigns of advocacy groups.

www.irb.gc.ca/eng/Pages/index.aspx

The page for the Immigration and Refugee Board, Canada, provides descriptions of the board's different programs, as well as instructions on how to apply for asylum in Canada.

http://refugees.org

The website of the U.S. Committee for Refugees covers refugee issues involving the United States and provides updates on the most recent developments of the committee.

http://www.worldrefugee.com

This website of the WorldNews Network is a source for the latest news and feature stories about refugees.

Publisher's Note: The websites listed on this page were active at the time of publication. The publisher is not responsible for websites that have changed their address or discontinued operation since the date of publication. The publisher reviews and updates the websites each time the book is reprinted.

http://www.lchr.org

The home site of the Lawyers Committee for Human Rights is an informative source, covering the organization's efforts to support refugees and other victims of persecution or repression.

http://www.unhcr.ch

The official site of the United Nations High Commissioner for Refugees gives updates on developments worldwide.

Index

1951 Convention Relating to the Status of
    Refugees, 40–41
1976 Immigration Act (Canada), 38
1952 Immigration and Nationality Act, 30
1965 Immigration and Nationality Act,
    20–21, 30–31, 42–43
1967 Protocol Relating to the Status of
    Refugees, 17, 41, 49, 52, 54

Africa, 20, *21*
*American Baptist Churches of the
    U.S.A. v. Meese* (*ABC* Case), 62–63
Amnesty International, 53, 79
    See also human rights
Aristide, Jean-Bertrand, 54–55, 56–57
    See also Haiti
Ashcroft, John, 57
asylees
    acceptance rates, in the United States, *18*,
        20, *21*, 22, 57, 59, 61, *95*
    definition of, 17, 49
    difficulties for, 83–85
    famous, 91–99
    policy regarding, 24–25, 38–41, 50–51,
        53–54, 57, 62–63, 87–89
    processing, 17, 22–24, 54–57, 65–67, 69,
        70–71, 75–81
        See also asylum reform; refugees
Asylum Corps, 54, 80
asylum reform, 66–73
    See also asylees

Baluchi, Reza, 97, *98*
Baryshnikov, Mikhail, *91*, 93
Bashir, Layli Miller, 95–96

Batista, Fulgencio, 45
Bay of Pigs invasion, 46–47
    See also Cuba
"boat people," 53–54
Borrego, Carlos, 98–99
Bosnia and Herzegovina, 15–16
Braun, Wernher von, 91–93
Brownell, Herbert, Jr., 41–42
Bureau of Citizenship and Immigration
    Services (BCIS), 21, 33
        See also Immigration and
            Naturalization Service (INS)
Bureau of Customs and Border Protection
    (BCBP), 33, 88
Bureau of Immigration and Customs
    Enforcement (BICE), 33, 88
Bush, George H. W., 54, 55
Bush, George W., 22, *32*, 57

Canada, 62, 89
    immigration history, 36–39
Carter, Jimmy, 49, 50–51
Castro, Fidel, 45, 48, 50
    See also Cuba
Central America, 59–63
China, *18*
Chinese Exclusion Act of 1882, 28
    See also ethnicity
civil war, 15–16, 60
Clinton, Bill, 57, 62–63, 65, 69, 73
cold war, 25, 41, 93
    See also communism
Colombia, *18*
Committee to Protect Asylum (CPA), 71
    See also asylum reform

Numbers in ***bold italic*** refer to captions.

communism, 25, 30, 37, 41, 45, 49, 59, 61, 93
    See also Soviet Union
Contras, 60
    See also Nicaragua
Convention Relating to the Status of Refugees (1951), 40–41
Cuba, **23**, 45–51, 57, **75**, **96**, 97, 98–99
    asylees and refugees from, 45–49, 50–51, 57
        See also Haiti
Cuban Adjustment Act (1966), 48
Cuban Missile Crisis, **47**

Department of Homeland Security, 32–33
    See also Immigration and Naturalization Service (INS)
Displaced Persons Act of 1948, 29, 40
    See also refugees
Dornberger, Walter, 91
Duvalier, François (Papa Doc), 51, **52**
    See also Haiti
Duvalier, Jean-Claude (Baby Doc), 51, **52**
    See also Haiti

economy (U.S.), 24, 39, 85
Egypt, 20, **21**
El Salvador, 59, 60–63
Ellis Island, **27**
Enhanced Border Security and Visa Entry Reform Act (2002), 32
Ethiopia, **18**
ethnicity, 28, 36–37
    and communities, **35**
expedited removal, 72–73, 76
    See also summary exclusion bill

family life, 84–85
female genital mutilation (FGM), 20, **21**, 94–96
    See also persecution, grounds of
Fermi, Laura, 29
Fife, John, 62
"freedom flights," 48
    See also Cuba

González, Elián, 96–97
Grant, Madison, 29
Guantánamo Bay, Cuba, 55, 56–57
Guatemala, 59, 60, 62–63

Haiti, 51–55, 56–57, **75**
    asylees and refugees from, 51–55, 56–57
        See also Cuba
Homeland Security Act of 2002, 32, 88
    See also Department of Homeland Security
Honduras, 60
human rights, 34, 53–54, 55, 62, 68
Human Rights Watch, 79
    See also human rights
humanitarians, 24–25
Hungarian Revolution (1956), 37, 41–42, 45
    See also communism

Illegal Immigration Reform and Immigrant Responsibility Act (1996), 32, **68**, 70, 73, 76
illegal migration, 75–77
    See also undocumented immigrants
immigration
    history of, in Canada, 36–39
    history of, in the United States, 27–36
    rates of, in the United States, 28, 29–30, 34
    See also asylees; refugees
Immigration Act of 1924, 29
Immigration Act of 1990, 31–32
Immigration Act of 1952 (Canada), 37
Immigration and Nationality Act (1952), 30
Immigration and Nationality Act of 1965, 20–21, 30–31, 42–43
Immigration and Naturalization Service (INS), 21, 31, 32–33, 52–53, 54, 66, 73, 87–88
    See also Asylum Corps
Immigration and Refugee Protection Act (Canada), 38–39
Immigration Reform and Control Act (1986), 31, 69
India, **18**

interdiction, 53–54, **56**, 57
   See also asylees
internally displaced people, 18
   See also refugees
interviews, asylum, 76–80
   See also asylees

Johnson, Lyndon, **31**

Kansi, Mir Aimal, 65
Kassindja, Fauziya, 20, 94–96
   See also female genital mutilation
     (FGM)
Kennedy, John F., 47
Korchnoi, Viktor, 93

Laughlin, Harry N., 28–29

Mali, 20, **21**
Mariel boatlift, **50**, **75**
   See also Cuba
Martin, David, 69
McCollum, Bill, 67
Miami, Fla., 46, **83**, **84**, 96
Montt, Efraín Rios, **59**, 60
   See also Guatemala
Morales, Andy, 98–99
Musalo, Karen, 95–96
   See also Kassindja, Fauziya
National Council of Churches (NCC), 52
   See also Haiti
Nicaragua, 59–60, **61**, 63
Nicaraguan Adjustment and Central
   American Relief Act (1997), 63
non-refoulement, 17
Nureyev, Rudolf, **91**, 93

Operation Paperclip, 92–93
Operation Pedro Plan, 46
   See also Cuba

Pearson, Lester, **36**, 37
   See also Canada
persecution, grounds of, 19–22, 34, 79–80
   See also asylees
points system, 38

See also Canada
policy, asylum, 24–25, 38–41, 50–51, 53–54,
   57, 62–63, 87–89
     See also asylees
processing, asylee, 17, 22–24, 54–57, 65–67,
   69, 70–71, 75–81
     See also asylees
Proclamation 3504, **47**
   See also Cuba
Protocol Relating to the Status of Refugees
   (1967), 17, 41, 49, 52, 54

quotas, 28–29, 30

Reagan, Ronald, 53–54, 60
reform, asylum, 66–73
   See also asylees
Refugee Act of 1980, 31, 49–50, 52, 54, 61
     See also refugees
Refugee Information Center (RIC), 80
   See also Asylum Corps
refugees, 29, 36, 37, 42–43, 45, 89
   attitudes toward, 24, 39
   camps, **78**
   definition of, 17–22, 41, 49
   and persecution grounds, 19–22
     See also asylees
resettlement, 22, 46
restrictionists, 24, 53

"safe third country" agreement, 89
   See also policy, asylum
Sanctuary movement, 62, 76
   See also Central America
Sandinistas, 59–60, **61**
   See also Nicaragua
Sarajevo, Yugoslavia, 15, **16**
Schrag, Philip, 68, 70, 71, 72, 73
September 11 attacks, 24, 32, 33, 87, 89
   See also terrorism
Simpson, Alan, 67–69, 70–71
Slattery, William, 66–67
Smith, Lamar, 70–71, 72
Somoza, Anastasio, 59, **61**
   See also Nicaragua
Soviet Union, 25, 41, **42**, 45, 47–48, 57, **91**,

93
    See also communism
St. Louis, 39–40
    See also refugees
Stettinius, Edward R., 91–92
Sudan, 20, *21*
summary exclusion bill, *67*, 68, 71–72
    See also asylum reform

Temporary Protected Status, 54
    See also asylees
Temporary Quota Act of 1921, 29
    See also quotas
terrorism, 24, 32, 33, 65, 66, 72, 87, 89
Togo, 20, 94

undocumented immigrants, 31, 32, 33, 34
United Nations, 17, 49
United Nations High Commisioner for
    Refugees (UNHCR), 40–41, 53, 54, 62
United States
    and the 1967 Protocol, 17, 41, 49, 52, 54
    asylee policy, 24–25, 39–41, 50–51,
        53–54, 57, 62–63, 87–89
    asylees accepted, *18*, 20, *21*, 22, 57, 59,
        61, *95*
    and Cuba, 46–51

economy, 24, 39, 85
and Haiti, 51–55, 56–57
immigration history, 27–36
immigration rate, 28, 29–30, 34
U.S. Coordinator for Refugee Affairs, 49
USA PATRIOT Act (2002), 32
USNS *Comfort*, 56
    See also Haiti

Vietnam War, 53–54
visas, 28, 31, 32, 33, 75, *87*
diversity, 35
von Braun, Wernher. *See* Braun, Wernher
    von

A Well-Founded Fear (Schrag), 68, 71
World Trade Center, 65, 66, 87, *88*, 97
    See also terrorism
World War I, 28
World War II, 28, 29, 37, 39–40

Yearbook of Immigration Statistics, 80
Yousef, Rasmzi Ahmed, 65
Yugoslavia, 15

Contributors

Senior consulting editor STUART ANDERSON is an adjunct scholar at the Cato Institute and executive director of the National Foundation for American Policy. From August 2001 to January 2003, he served as executive associate commissioner for Policy and Planning and Counselor to the Commissioner at the Immigration and Naturalization Service. He spent four and a half years on Capitol Hill on the Senate Immigration Subcommittee, first for Senator Spencer Abraham and then as Staff Director of the subcommittee for Senator Sam Brownback. Prior to that, Stuart was Director of Trade and Immigration Studies at the Cato Institute, where he produced reports on the military contributions of immigrants and the role of immigrants in high technology. Stuart has published articles in the Wall Street Journal, New York Times, Los Angeles Times, and other publications. He has an M.A. from Georgetown University and a B.A. in Political Science from Drew University. His articles have appeared in such publications as the *Wall Street Journal*, *New York Times*, and *Los Angeles Times*.

MARIAN L. SMITH served as the senior historian of the U.S. Immigration and Naturalization Service (INS) from 1988 to 2003, and is currently the immigration and naturalization historian within the Department of Homeland Security in Washington, D.C. She studies, publishes, and speaks on the history of the immigration agency and is active in the management of official 20th-century immigration records.

PETER HAMMERSCHMIDT is director general of national cyber security at Public Safety Canada. He previously served as First Secretary (Financial and Military Affairs) for the Permanent Mission of Canada to the United Nations. Before taking this position, he was a ministerial speechwriter and policy specialist for the Department of National Defence in Ottawa. Prior to joining the public service, he served as the Publications Director for the Canadian Institute of Strategic Studies in Toronto. He has a B.A. (Honours) in Political Studies from Queen's University, and an MScEcon in Strategic Studies from the University of Wales, Aberystwyth.

FRANK WRIGHT is a freelance writer and editor. He was born in Union Township, New Jersey, and graduated from Ryder University. He currently lives in New York City with his wife and two children. This is his first book.

Picture Credits

Page

1: Ververidis Vasilis / Shutterstock.com
2: Jazzmany / Shutterstock.com
9: used under license from Shutterstock, Inc.
12: Stacey Newman / Shutterstock.com
14: Volodymyr Borodin / Shutterstock.com
17: Sergey Kohl / Shutterstock.com
21: Webistan/Corbis
25: U.S. Coast Guard
26: A. Katz / Shutterstock.com
28: Library of Congress
33: courtesy Lyndon B. Johnson Library
37: Hulton/Archive/Getty Images
39: United Nations photo
40: Hulton/Archive/Getty Images
42: Hulton/Archive/Getty Images
46: courtesy John F. Kennedy Library
48: Tim Chapman/Miami Herald/Getty Images
50: Hulton/Archive/Getty Images
54: United Nations photo
56: U.S. Coast Guard
58: Orlando Sierra/AFP/Getty Images
61: Hulton/Archive/Getty Images
63: United Nations photo
64: United Nations photo
68: Stephen Ferry/Liaison/Getty Images
71: Chris Kleponis/Getty Images
72: Christopher Ruppel/Getty Images
76: Orlok / Shutterstock.com
78: U.S. Department of Defense
83: U.S. Coast Guard
88: Joe Raedle/Getty Images
93: Anthony Correia / Shutterstock.com
95: National Aeronautics and Space
96: Hulton/Archive/Getty Images
99: Anthony Correia / Shutterstock.com
100: used under license from Shutterstock, Inc.